THE OFFICIAL

MINECRAFT

COLORING BOOK

Create, Explore, Relax

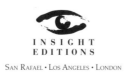

INSIGHT
EDITIONS

SAN RAFAEL · LOS ANGELES · LONDON

Dear Adventurer,

You have spent countless hours mining, building, and exploring the Minecraft world and have honed your creative skills to epic proportions. So, after surviving a harrowing night of hostile mobs, it's time for you to sit back, relax, and use your imagination to color something truly amazing. Inside the pages of this book, you will find familiar characters, mobs, blocks, weapons, armor, and biomes that can be shaped into works of Minecraft art—by you! Oh, Adventurer, your task will not be an easy one. You will encounter creeper attacks, a zombie horde, and even the Ender Dragon. Fear not, though—you have your trusty diamond sword and colored pencils to fend off those hostiles and boss mobs. So, sharpen up your favorite weapons, engage your creativity, and bravely go color without limits!

Sincerely,
The Guide

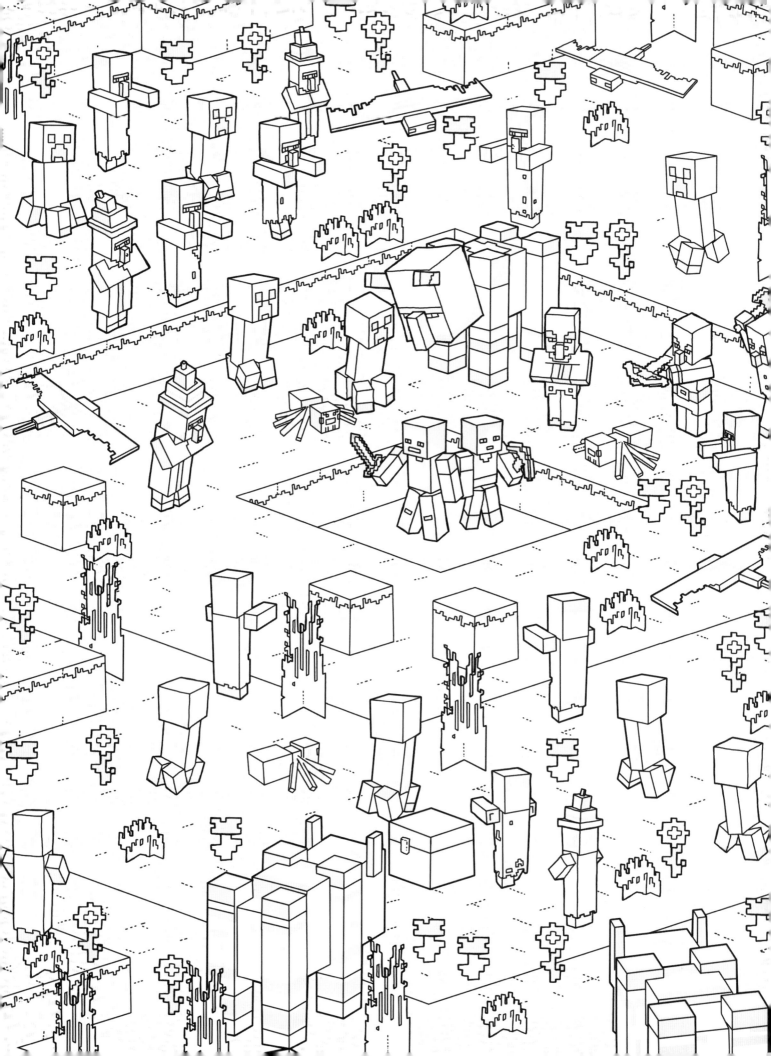

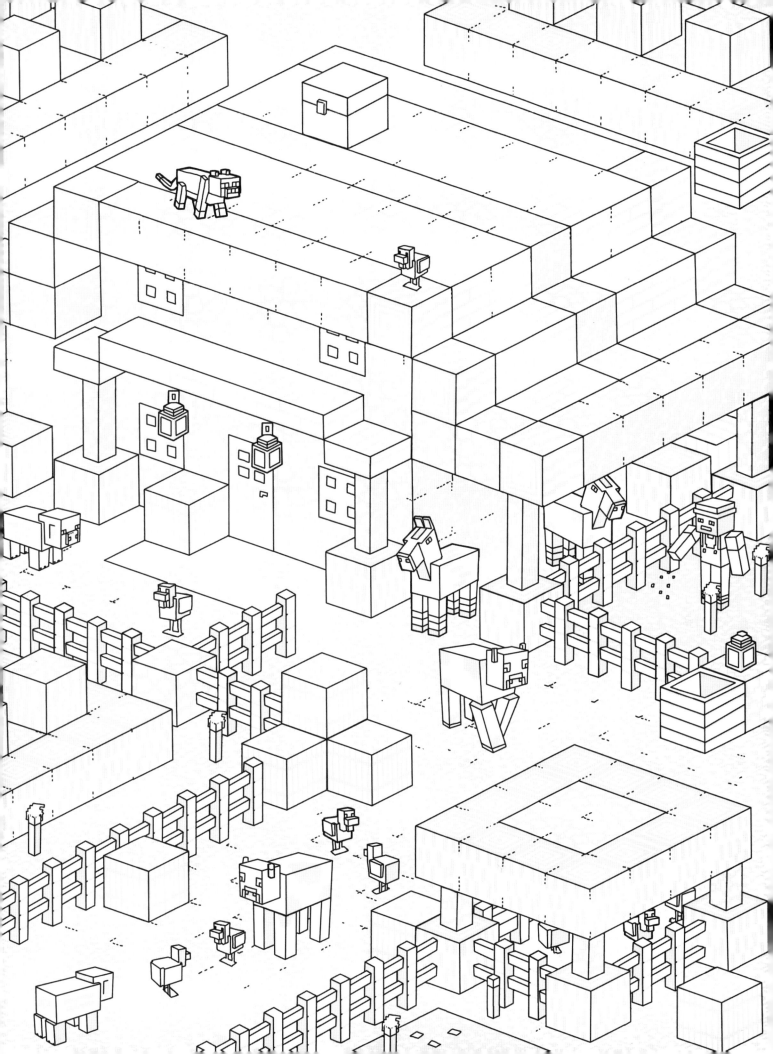

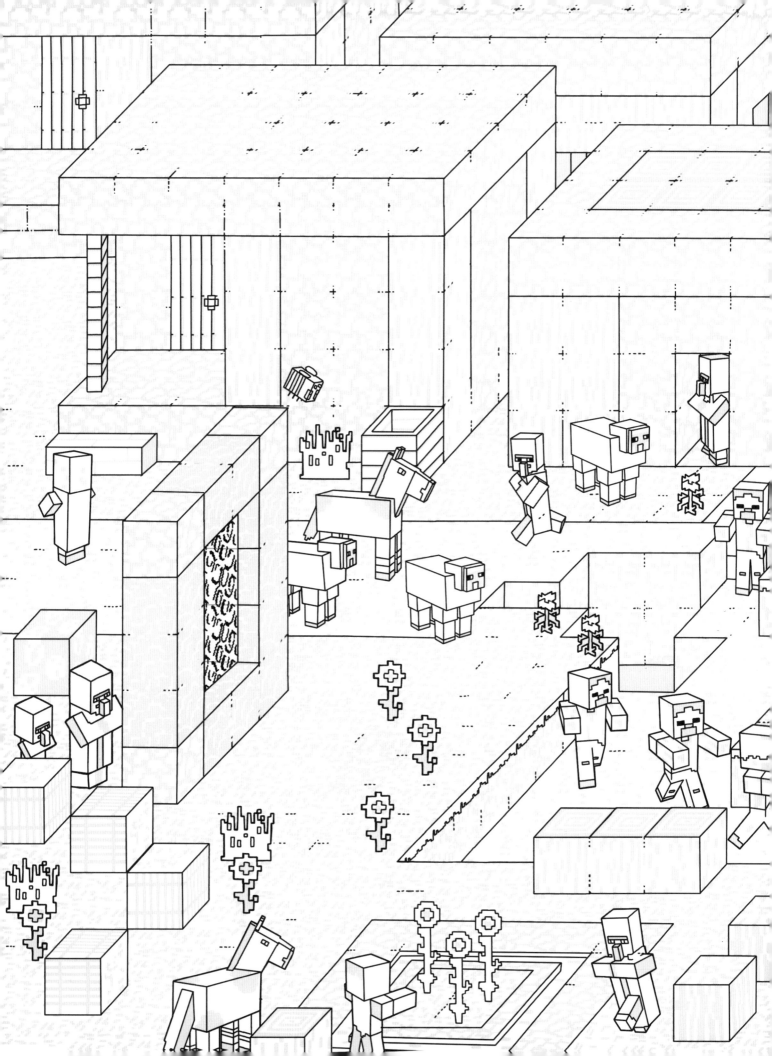

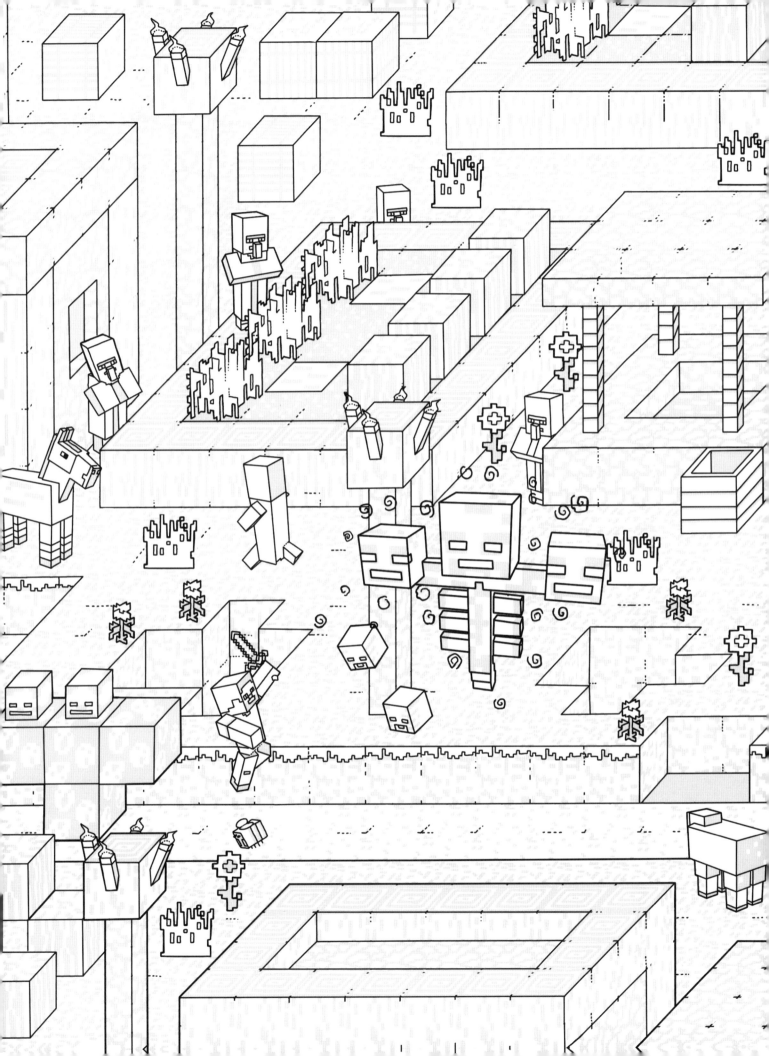

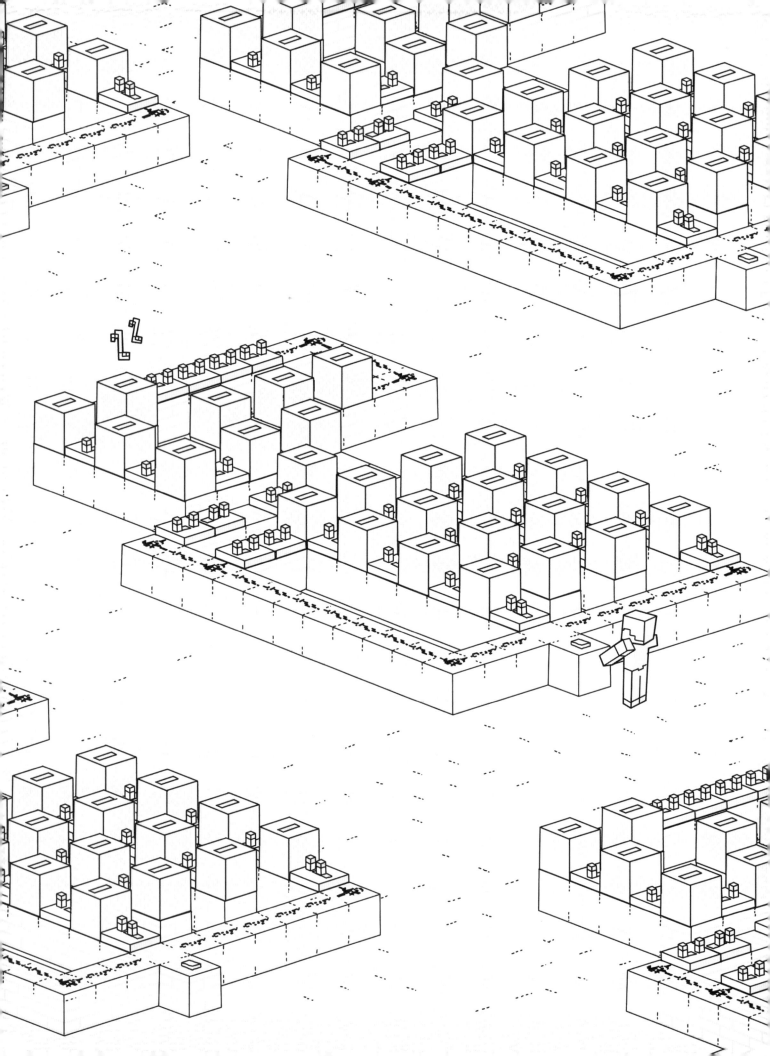

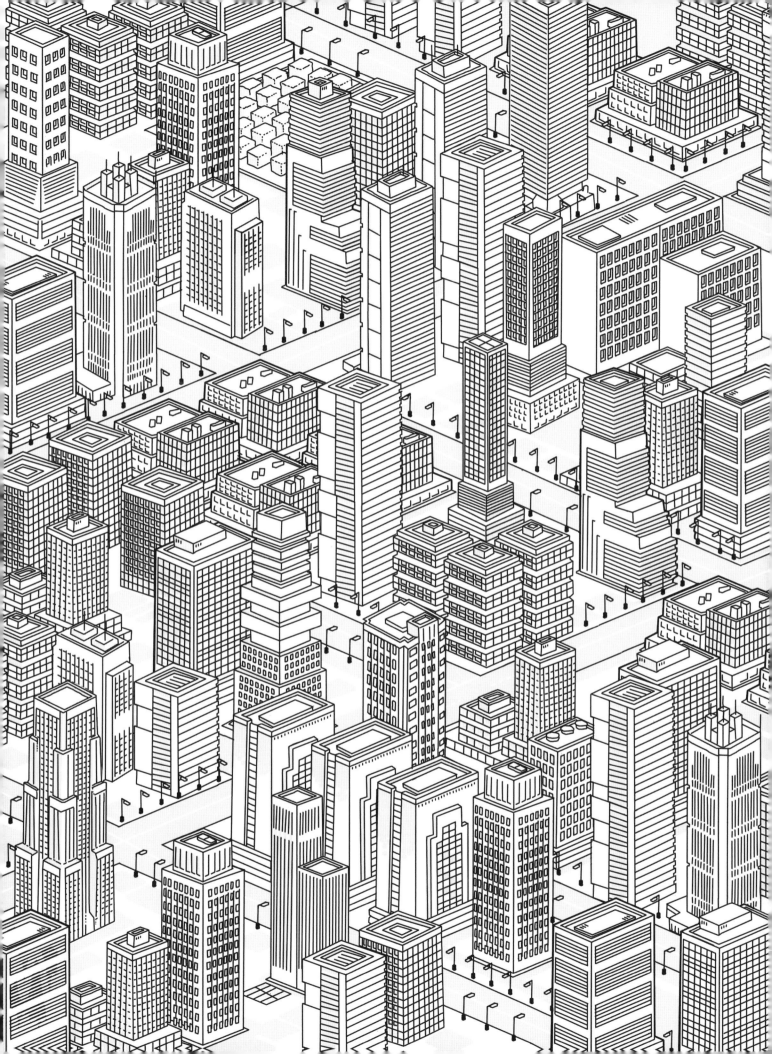

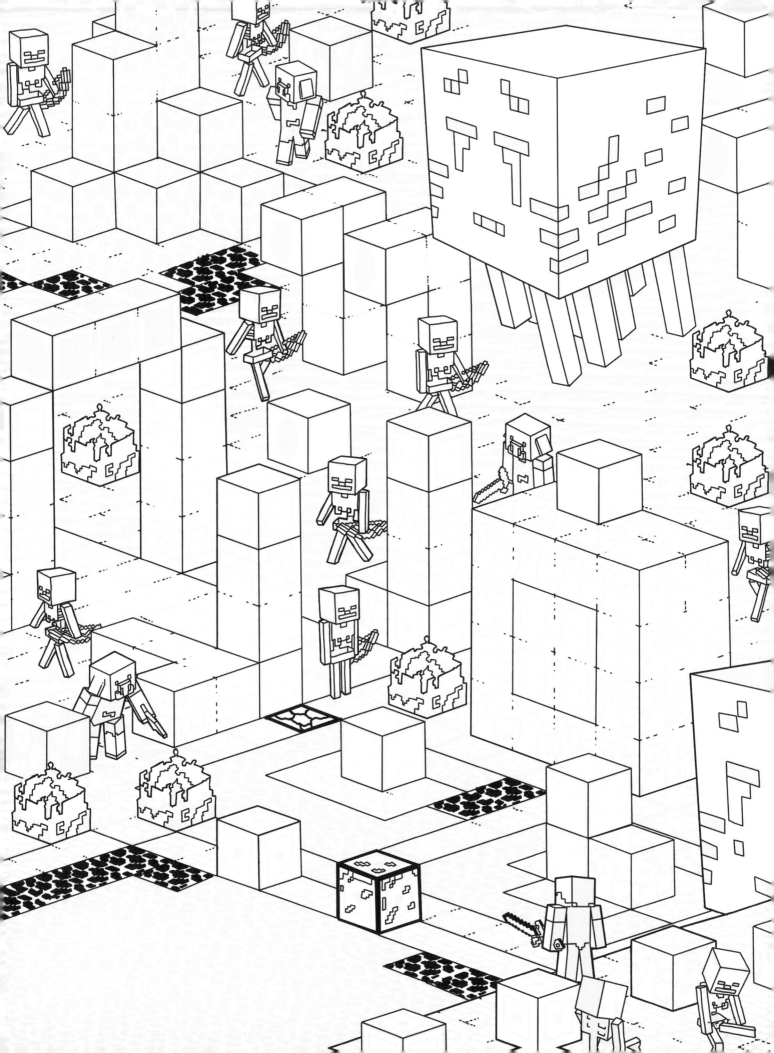

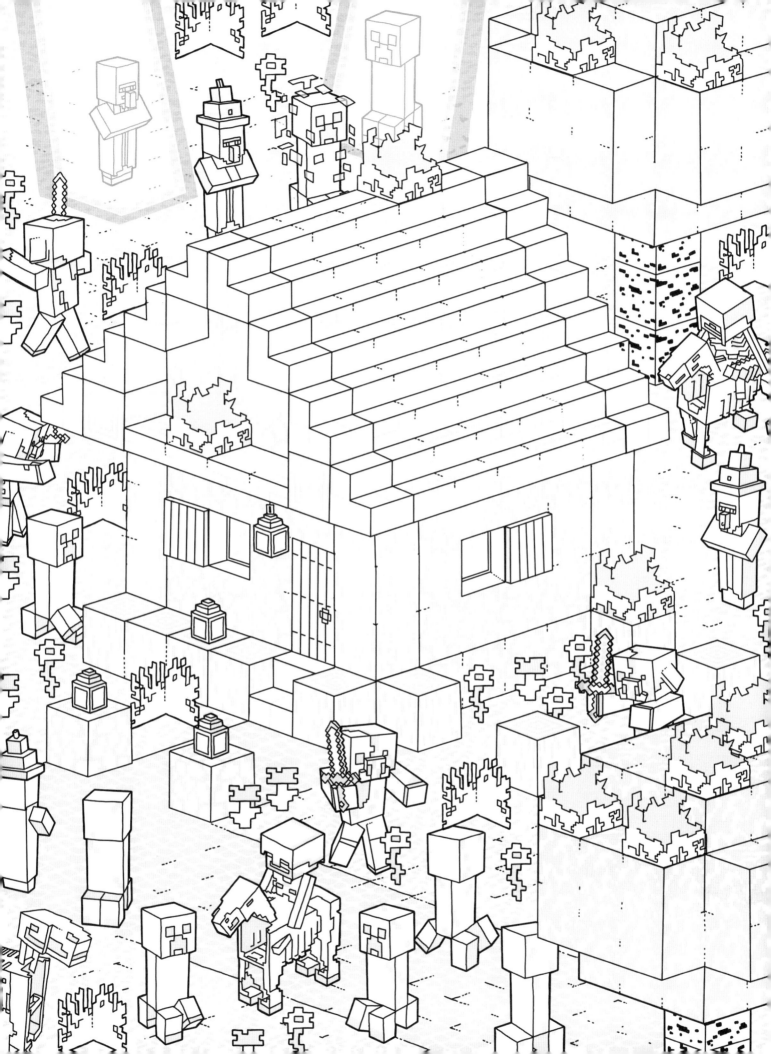

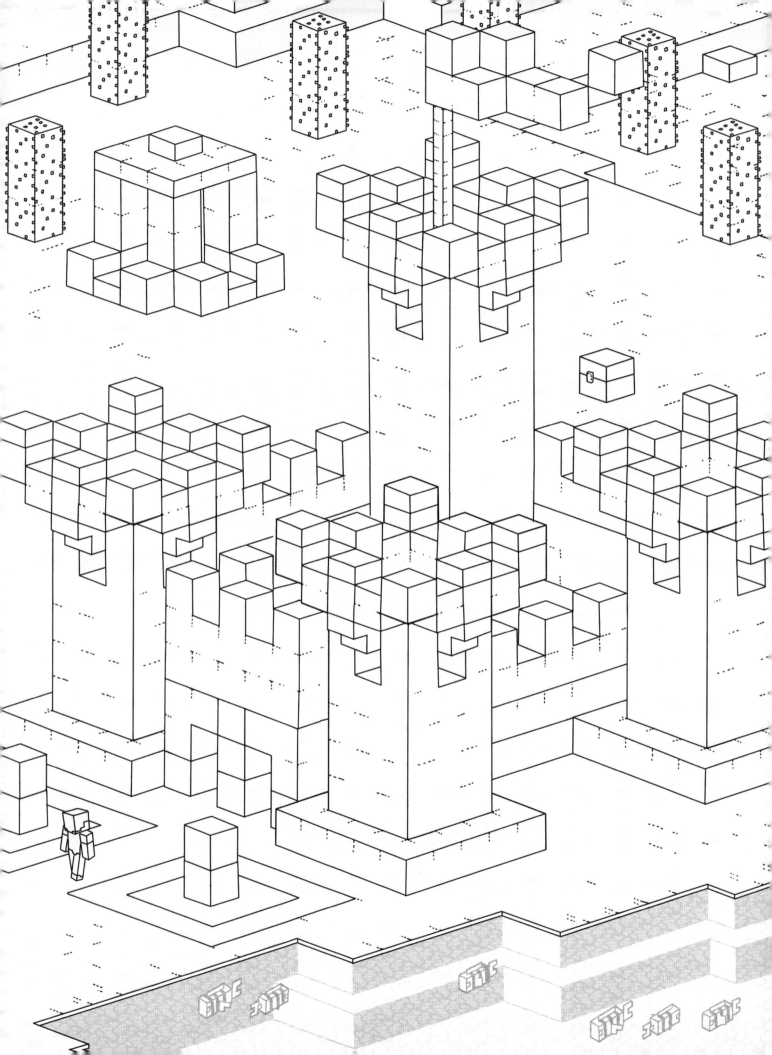

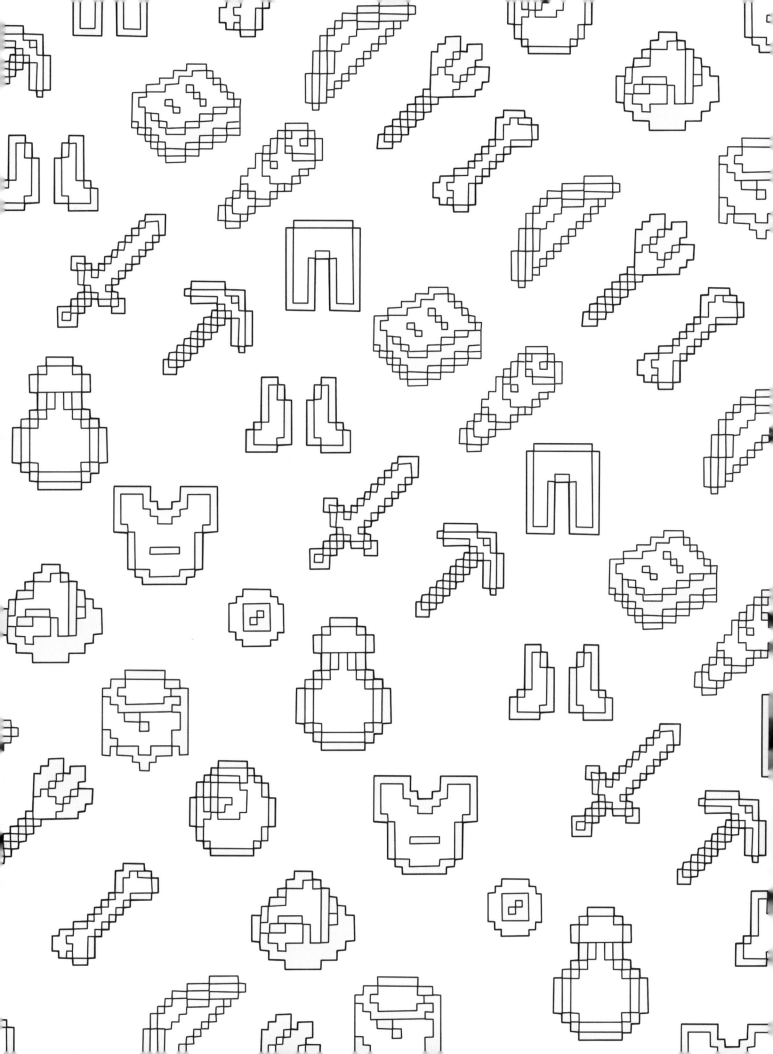

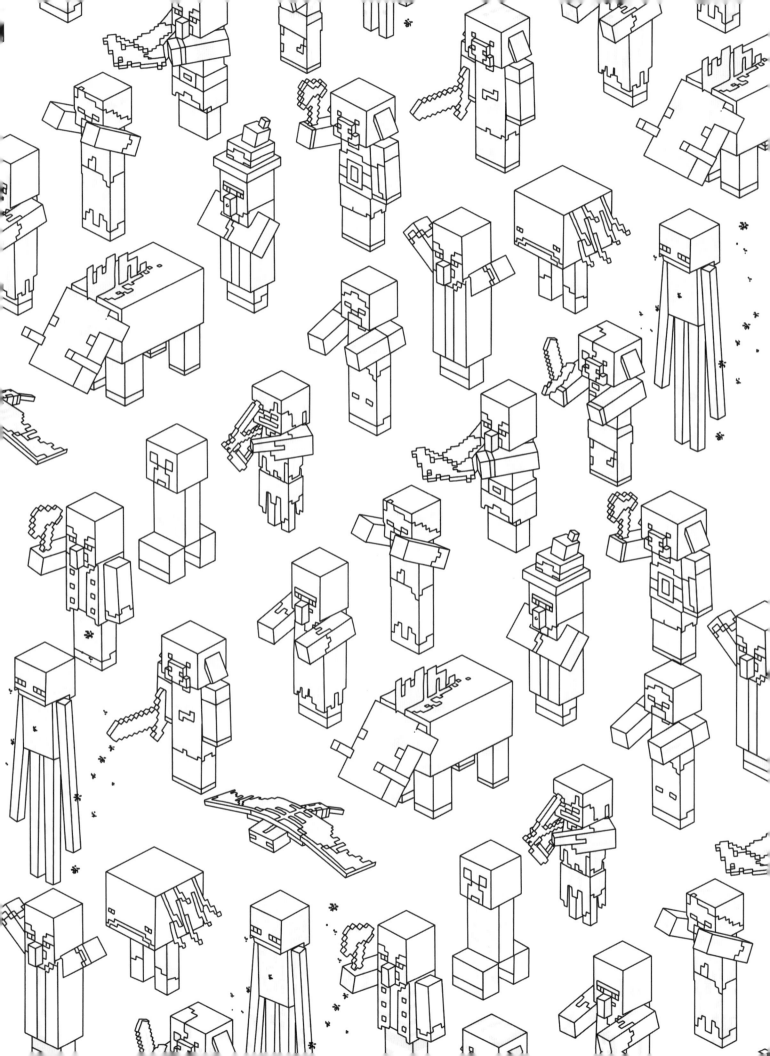

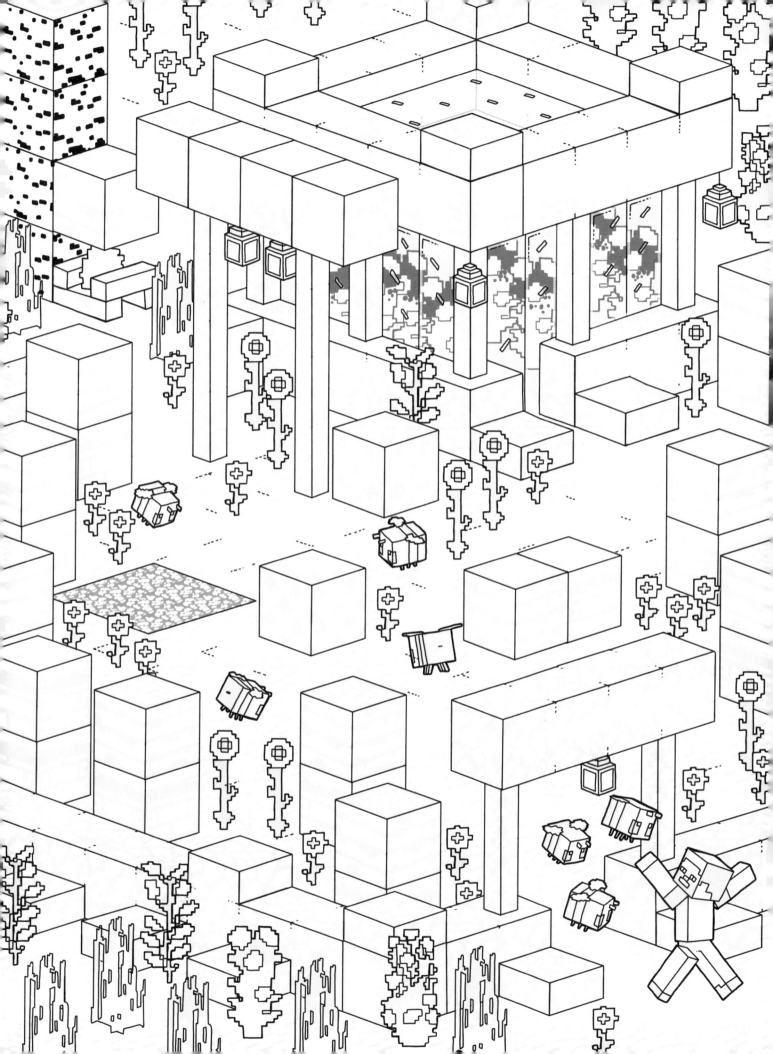

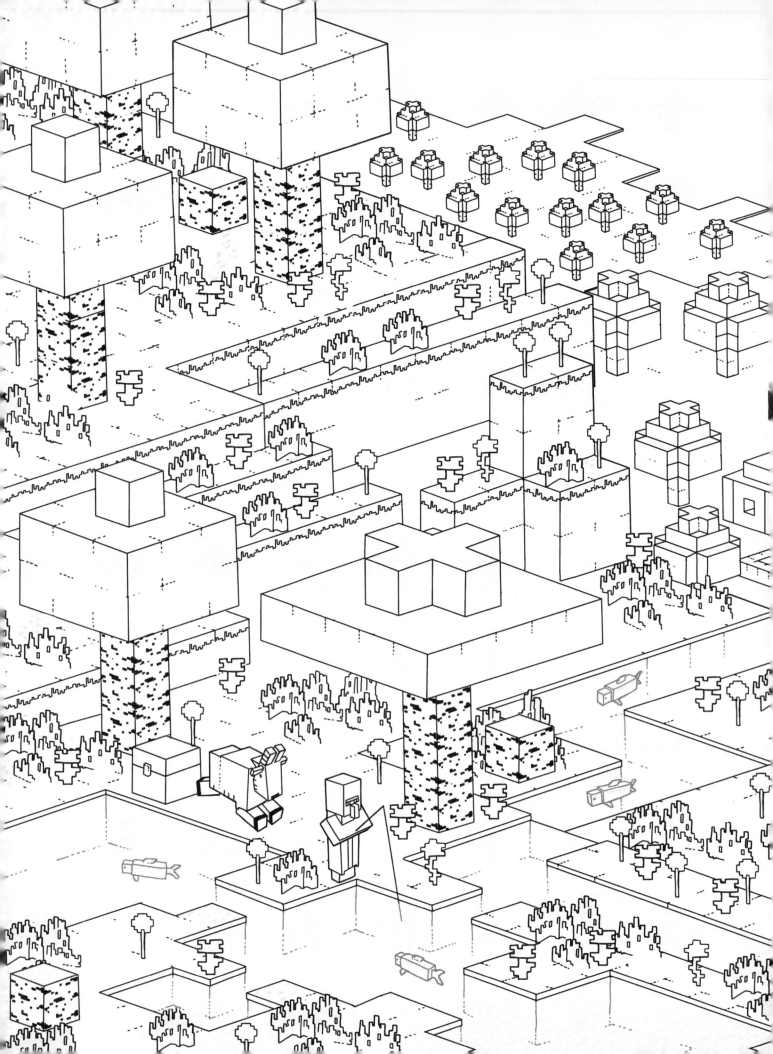

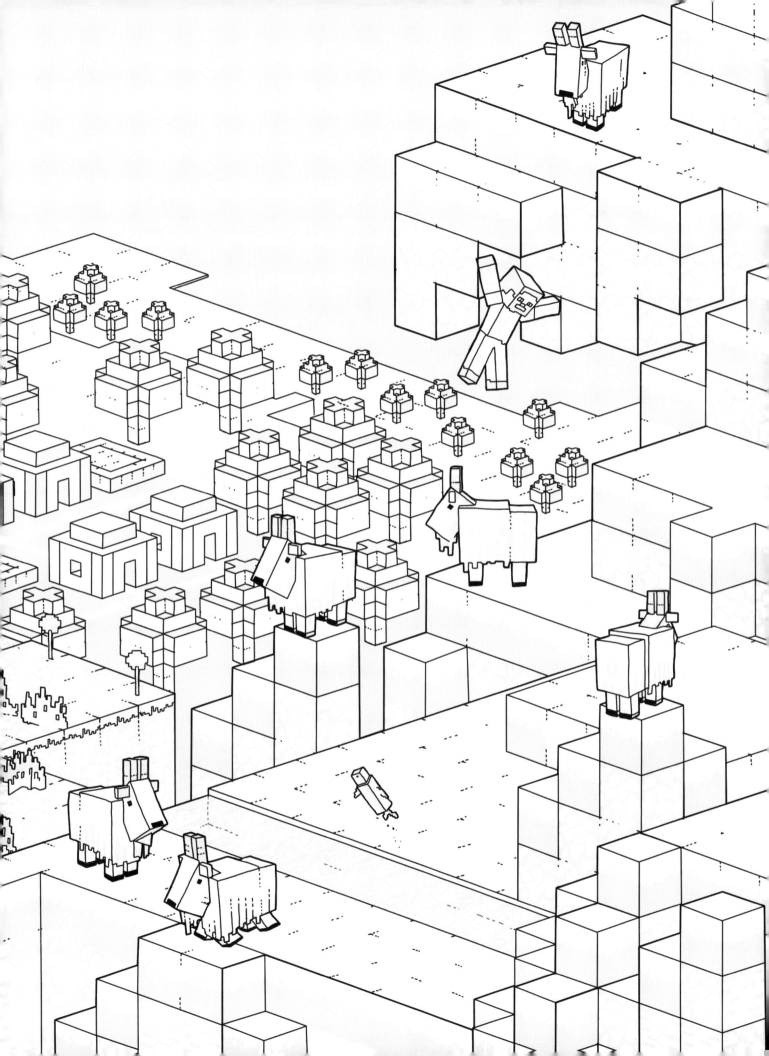

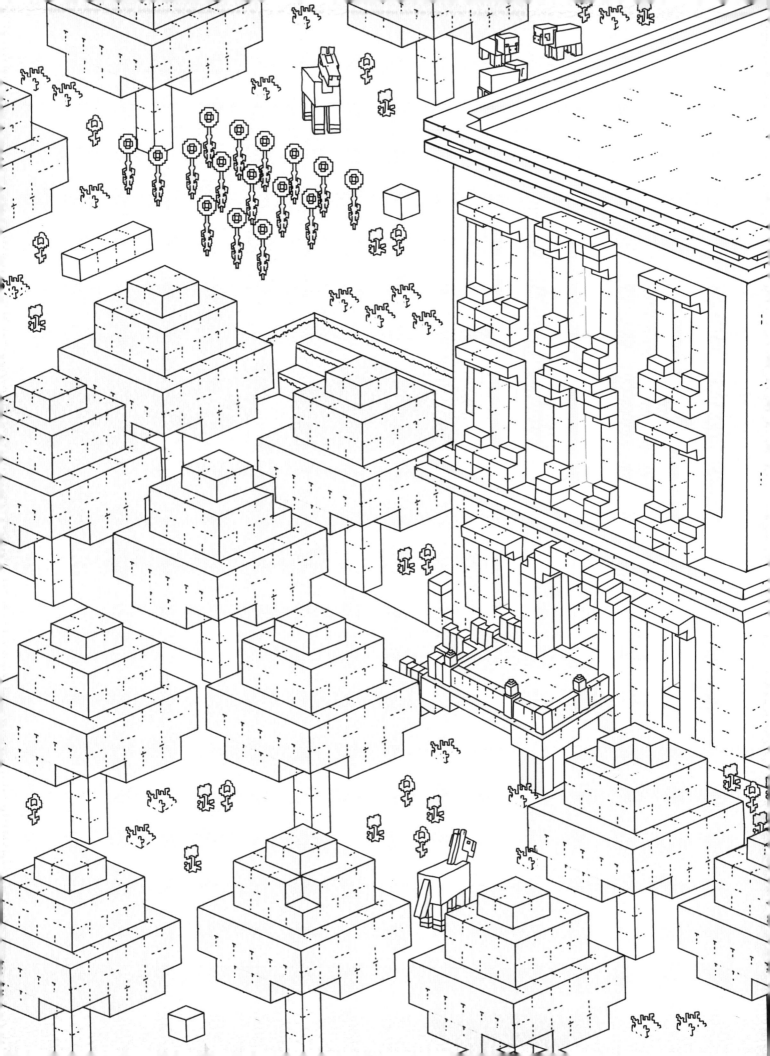

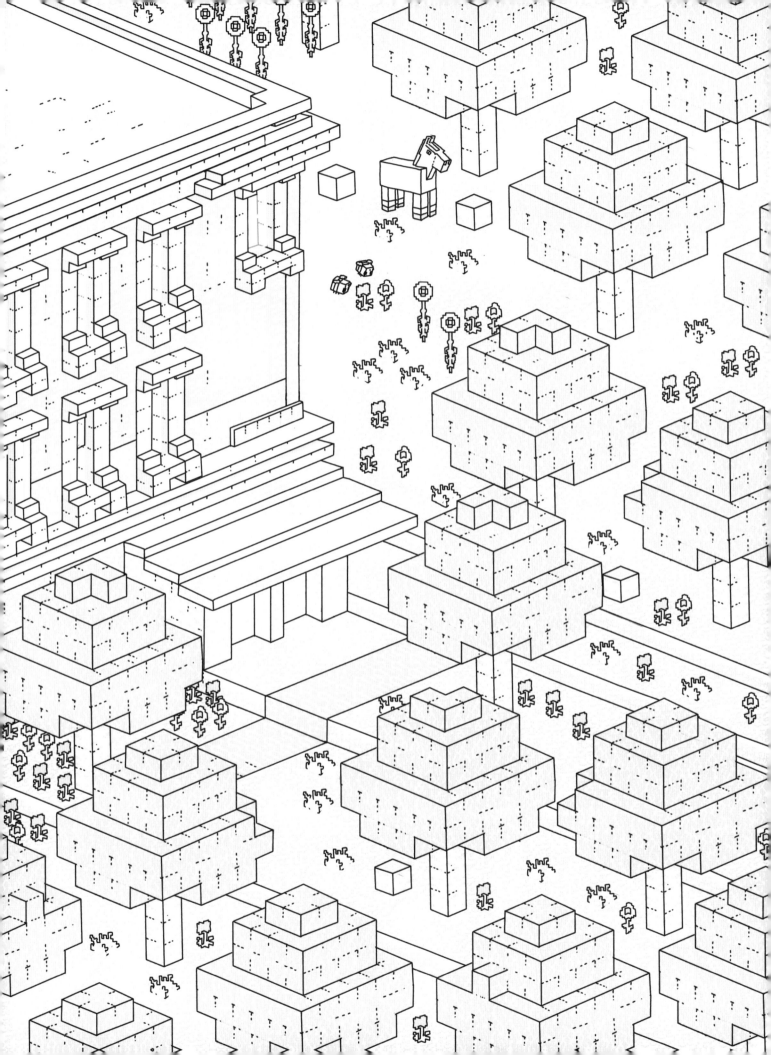

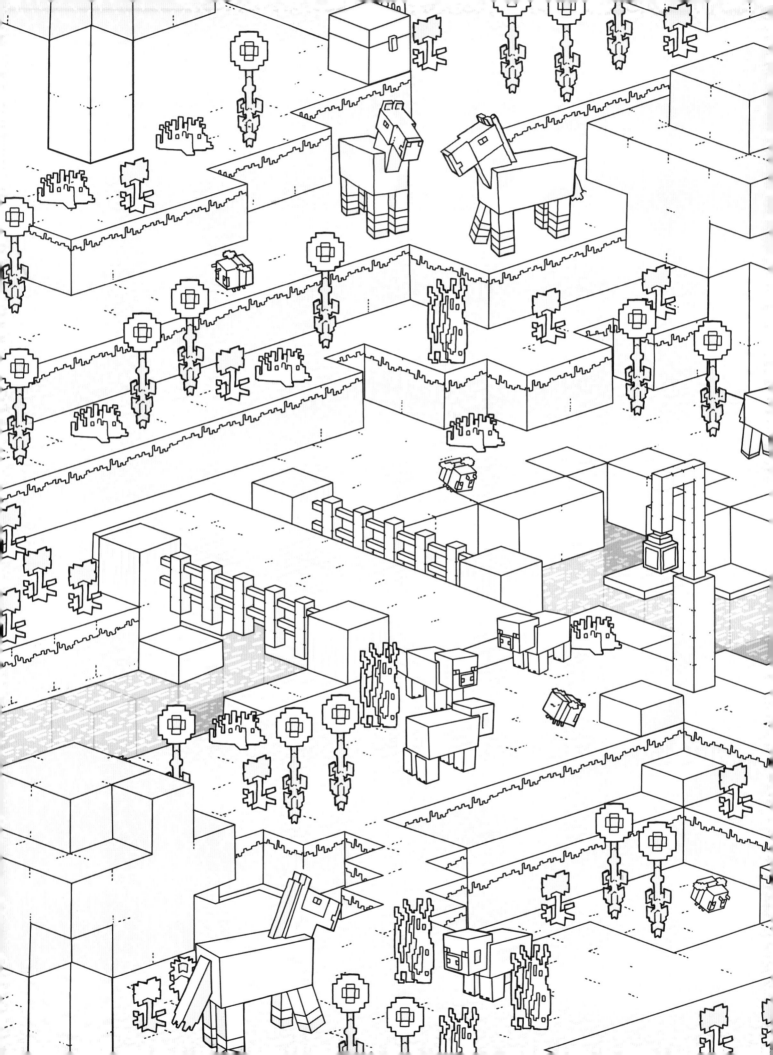

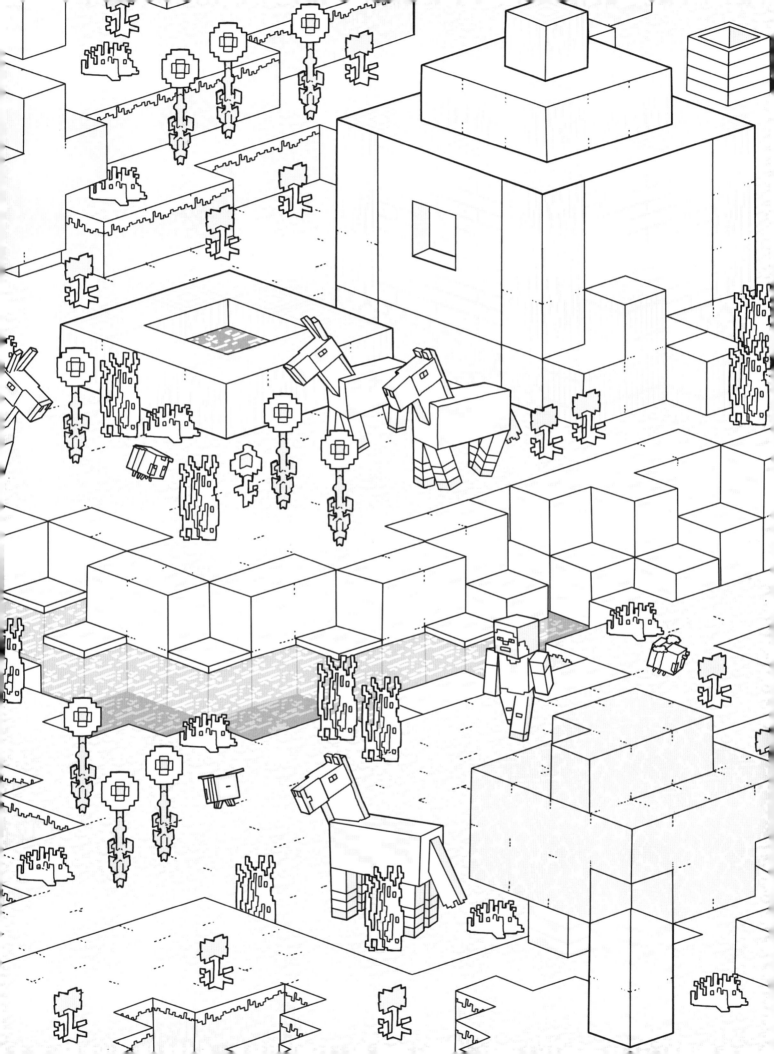

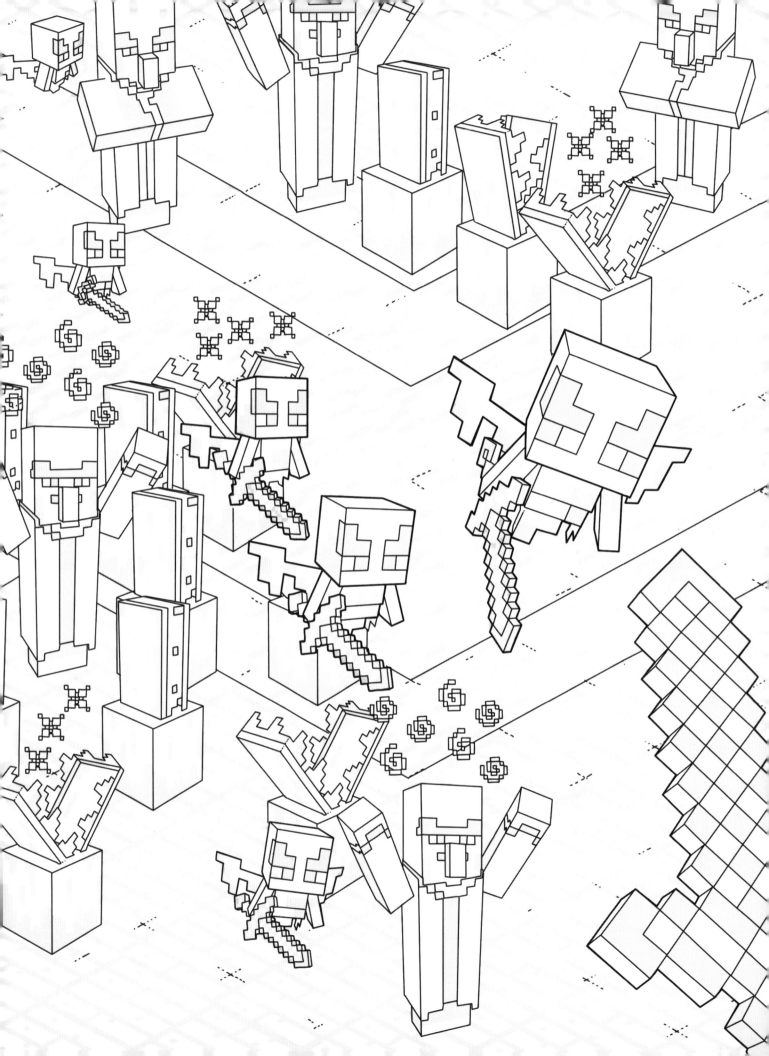

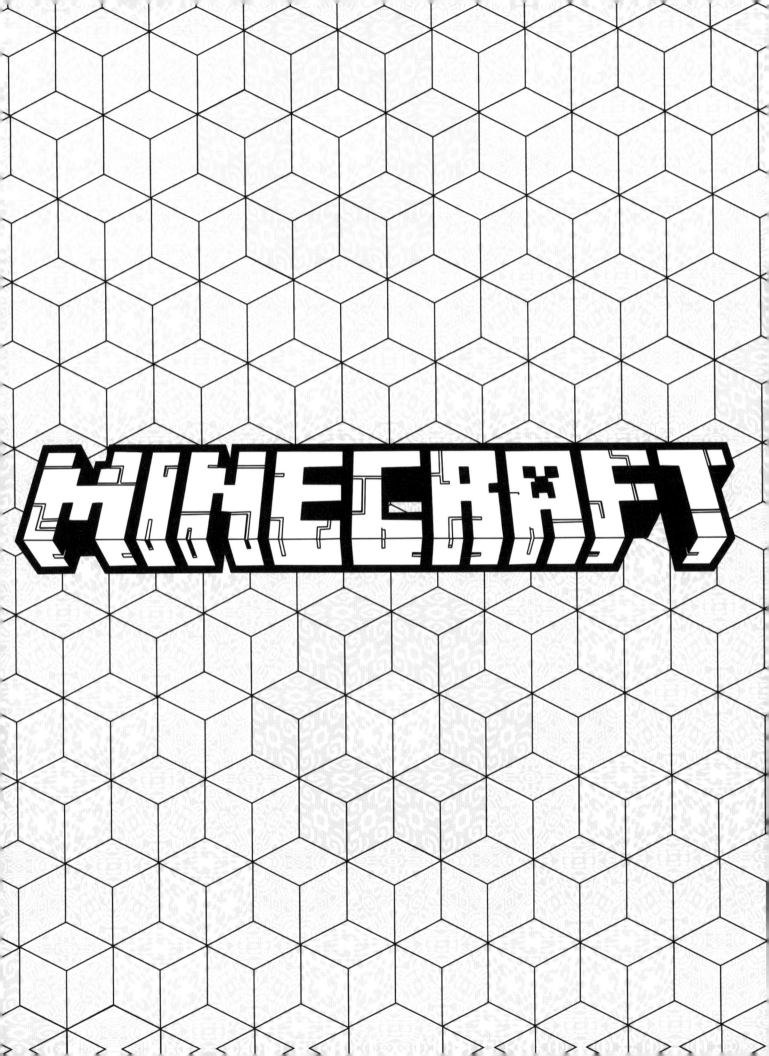

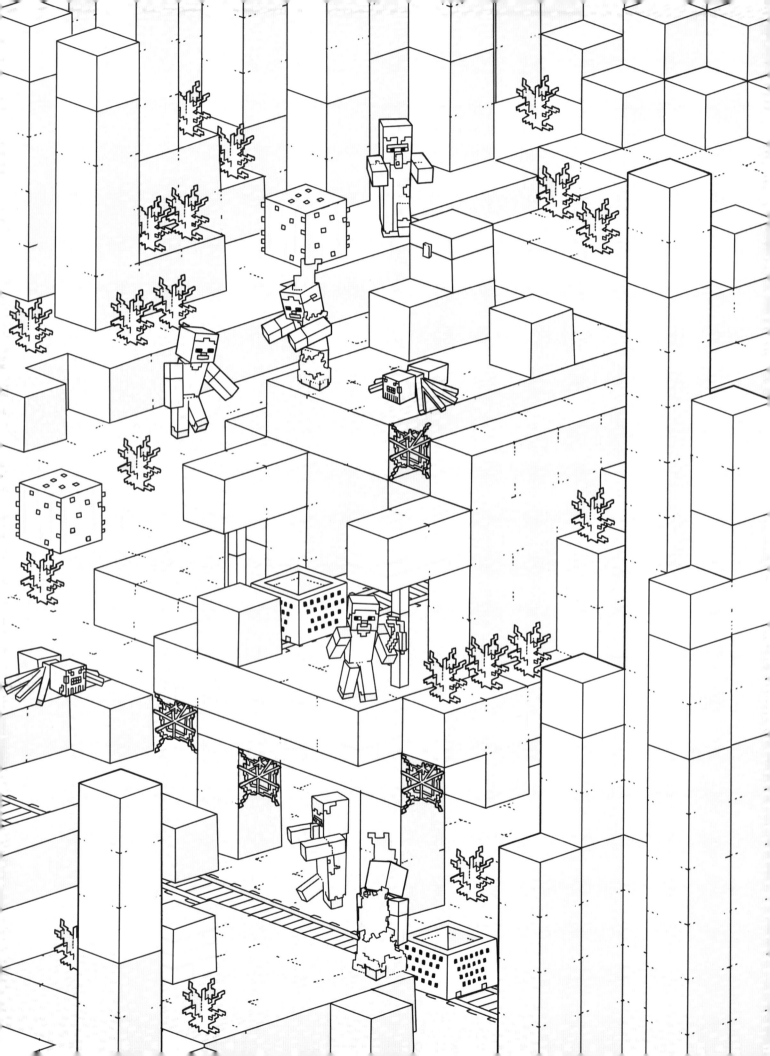

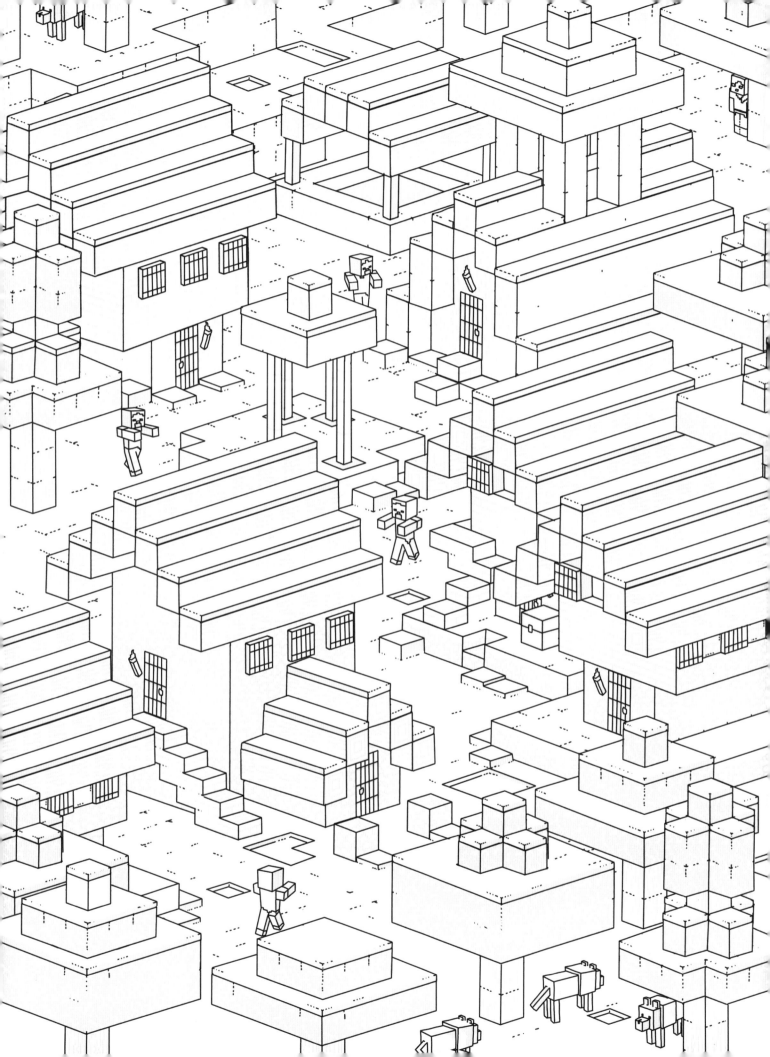

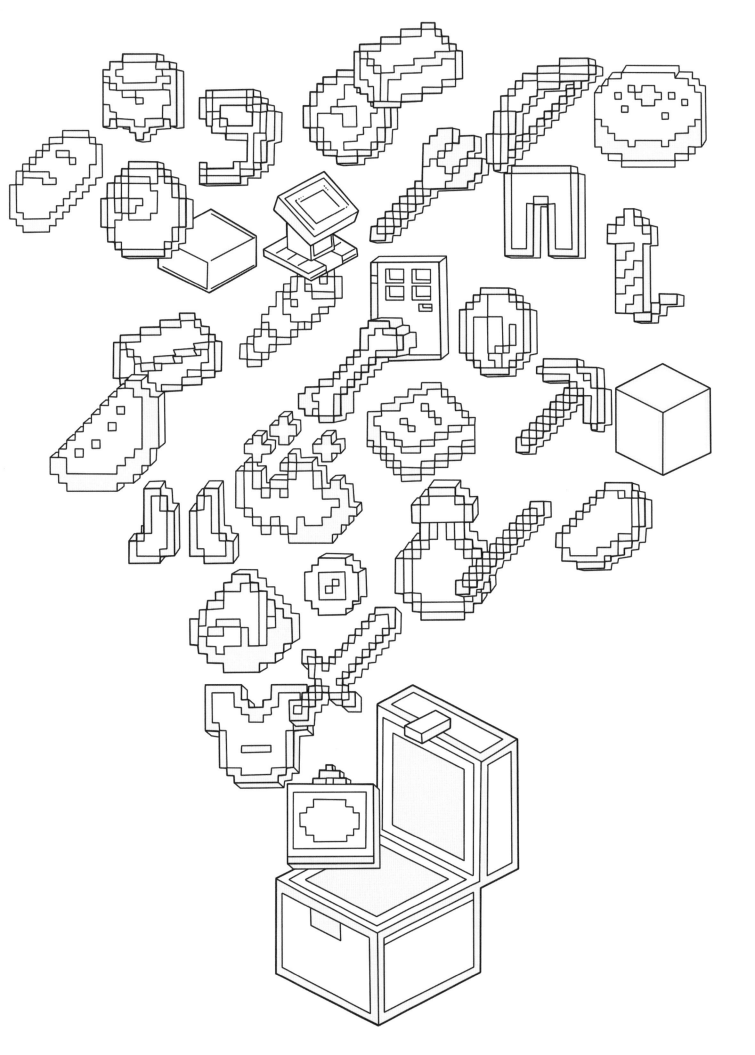

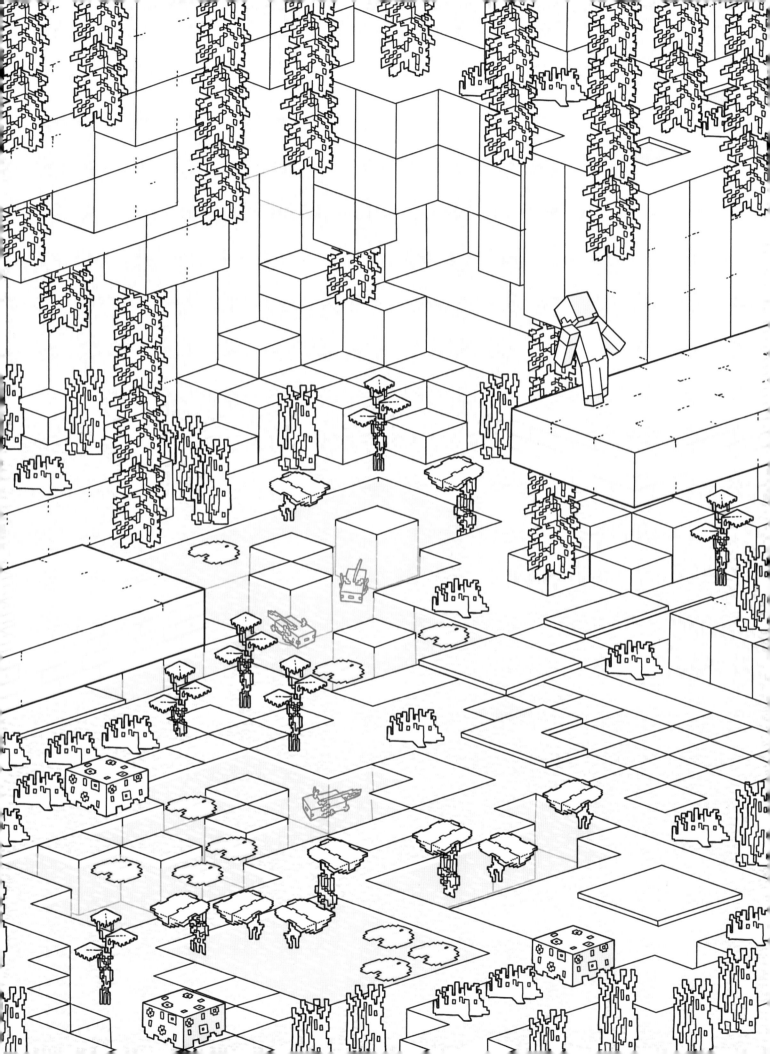

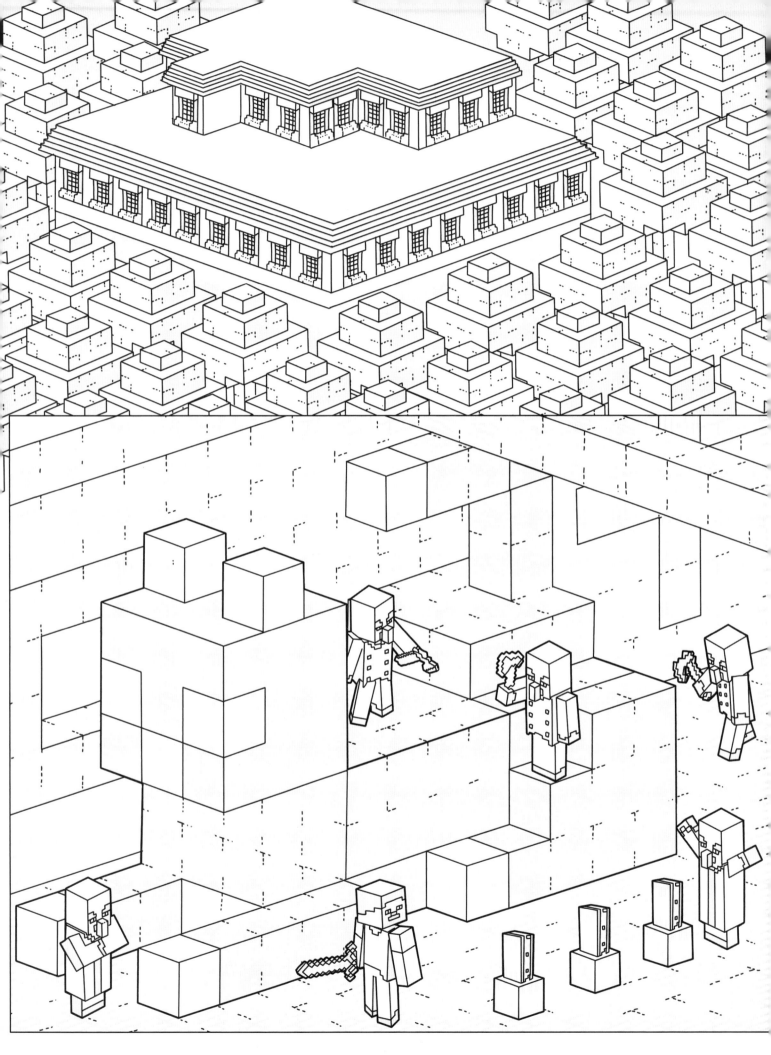

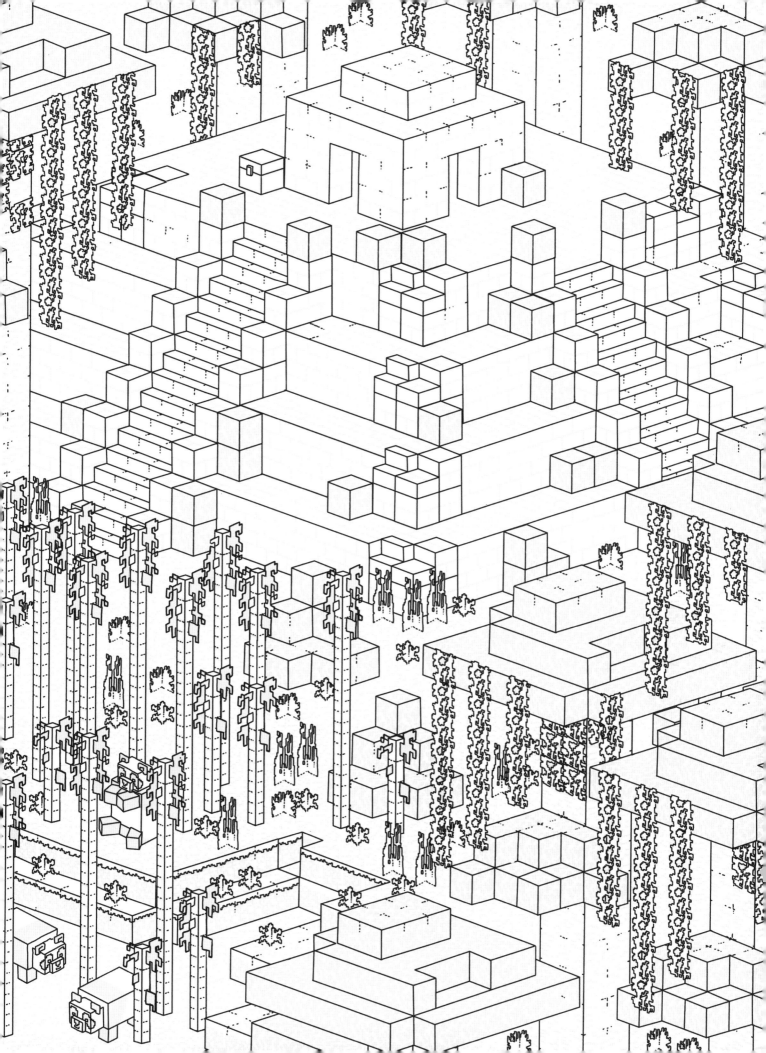

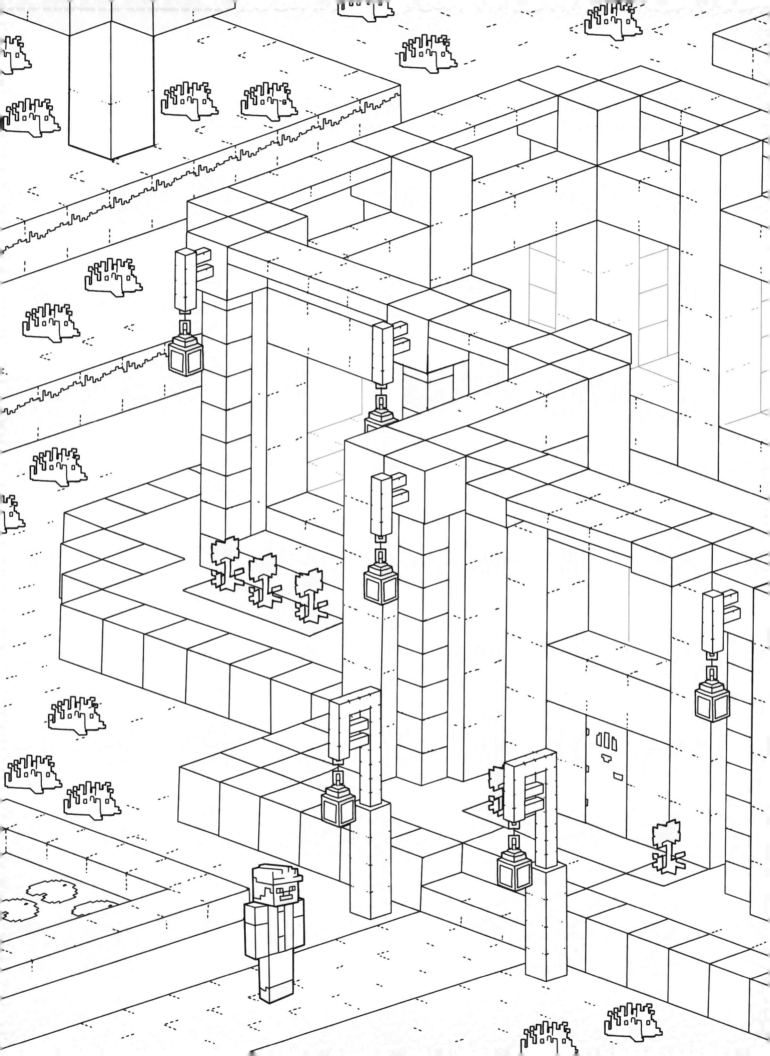

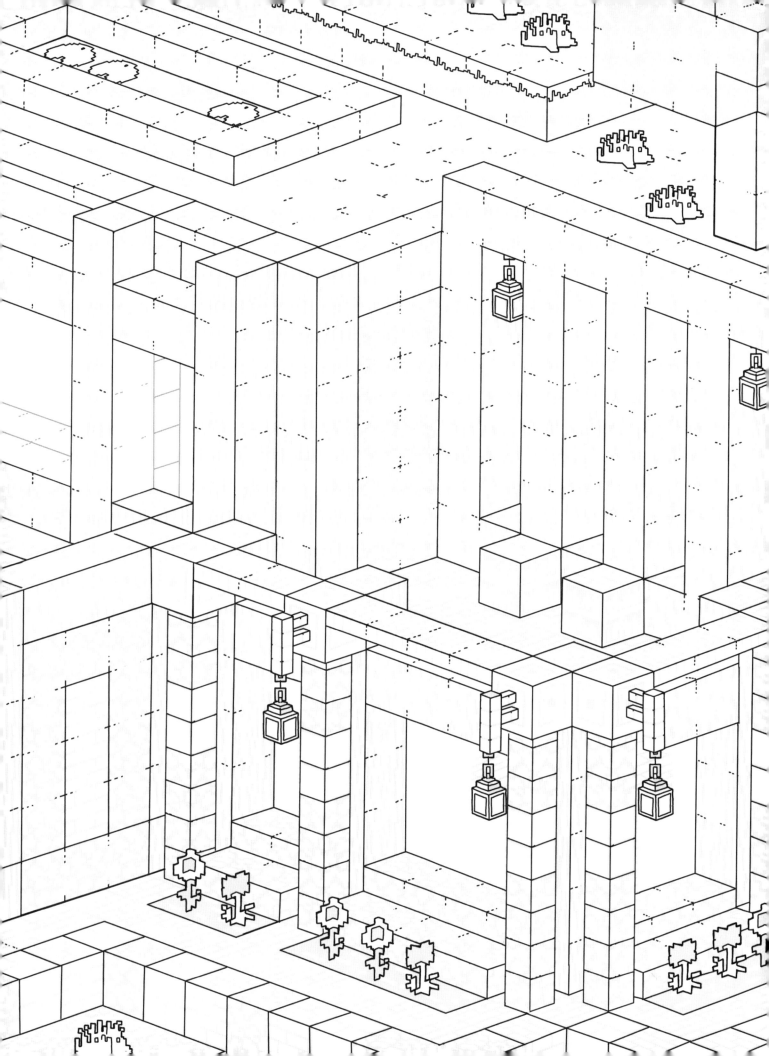

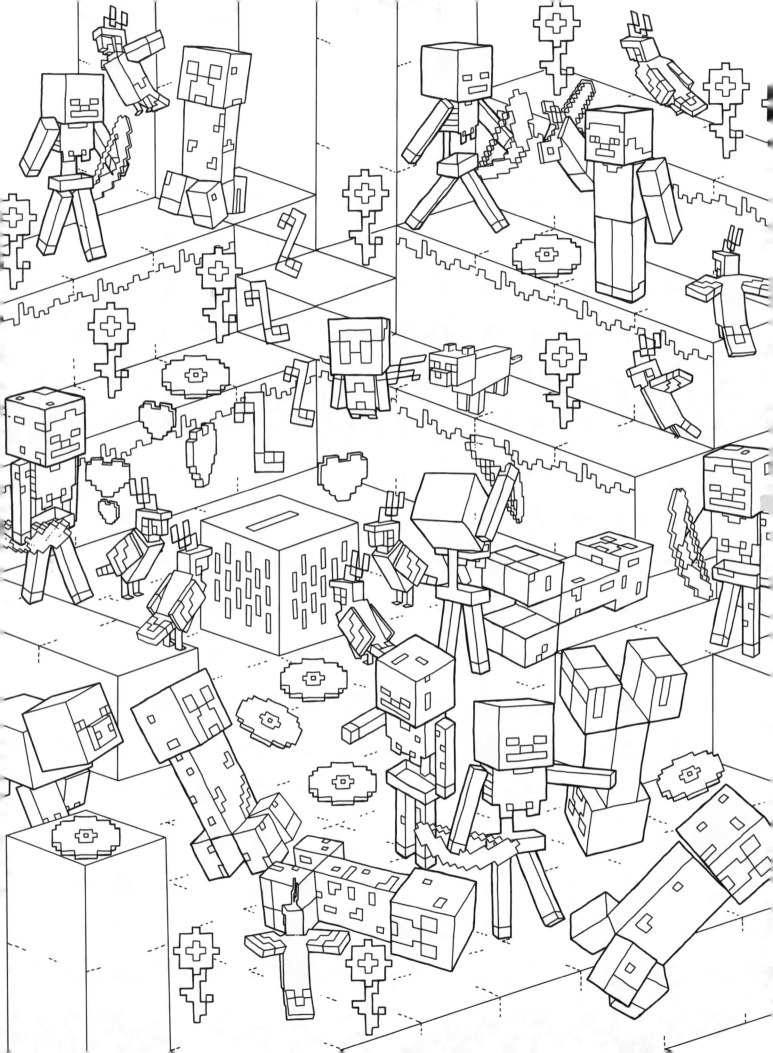

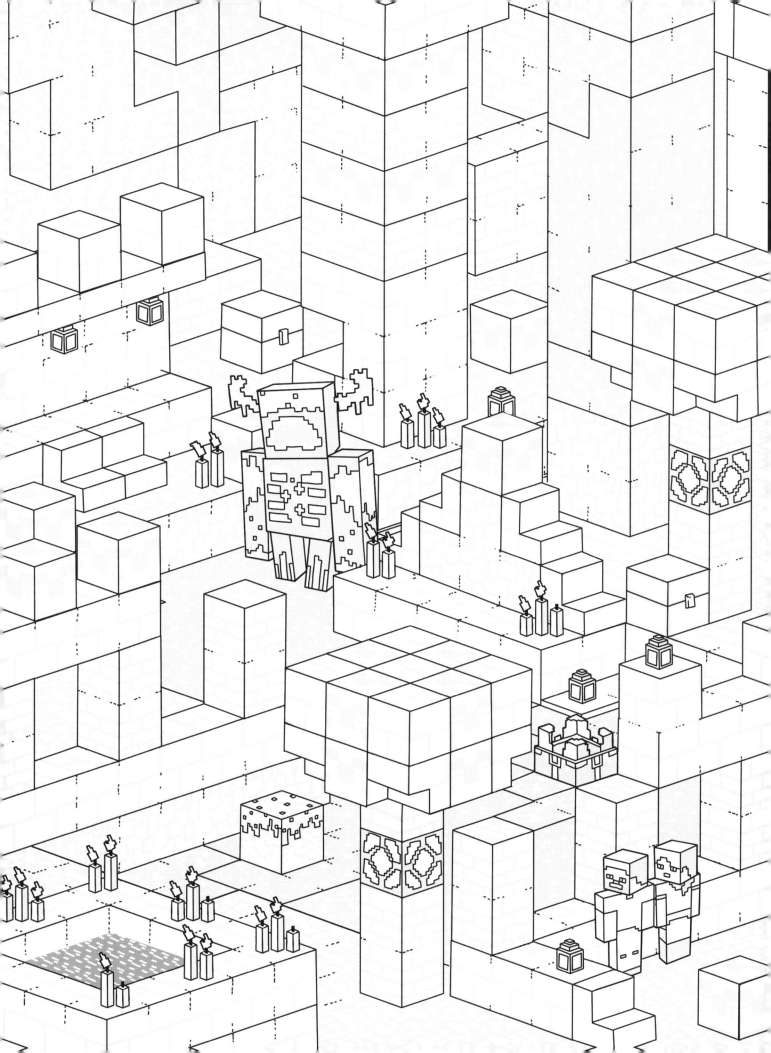

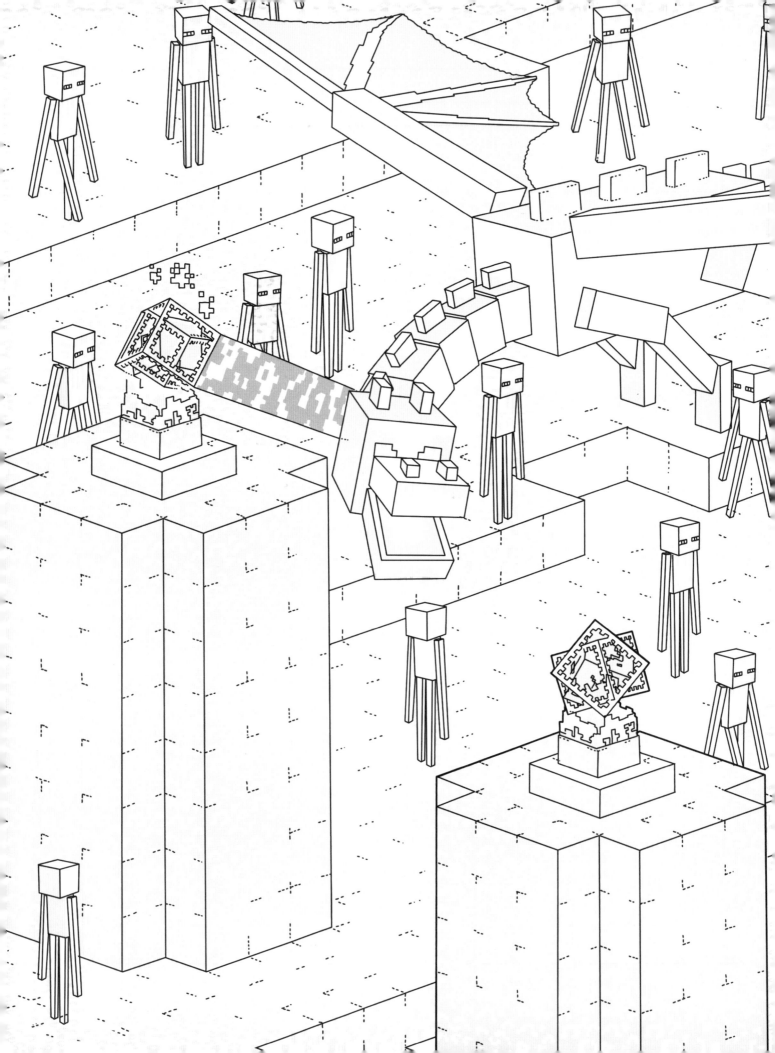

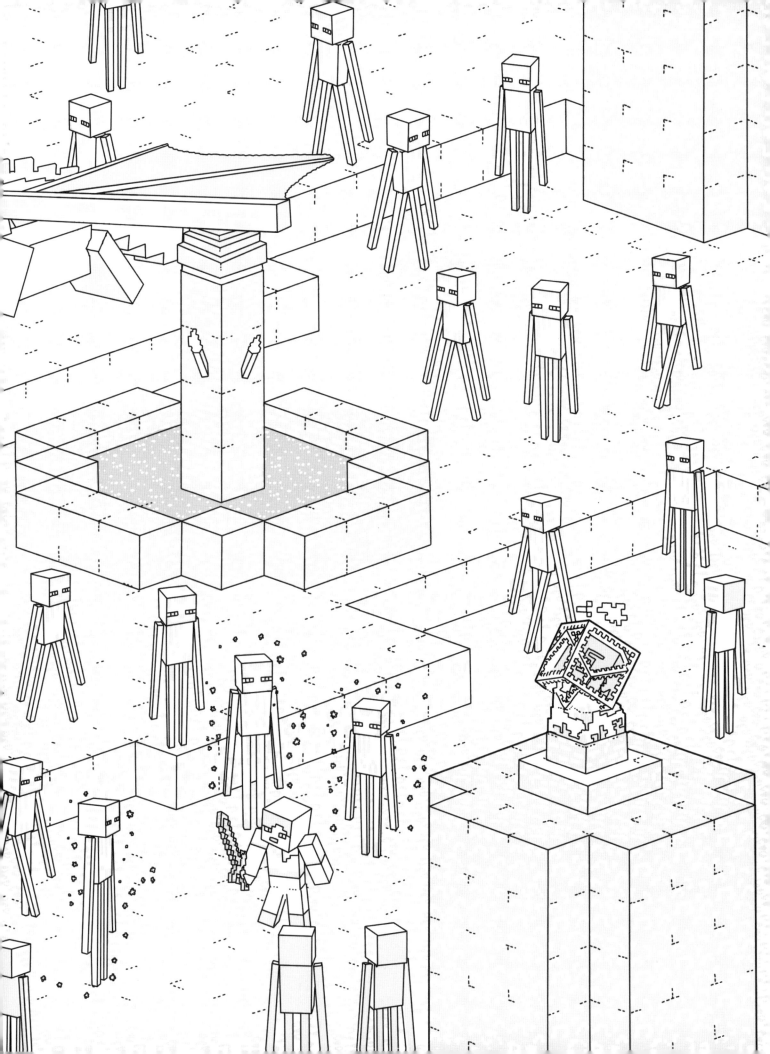

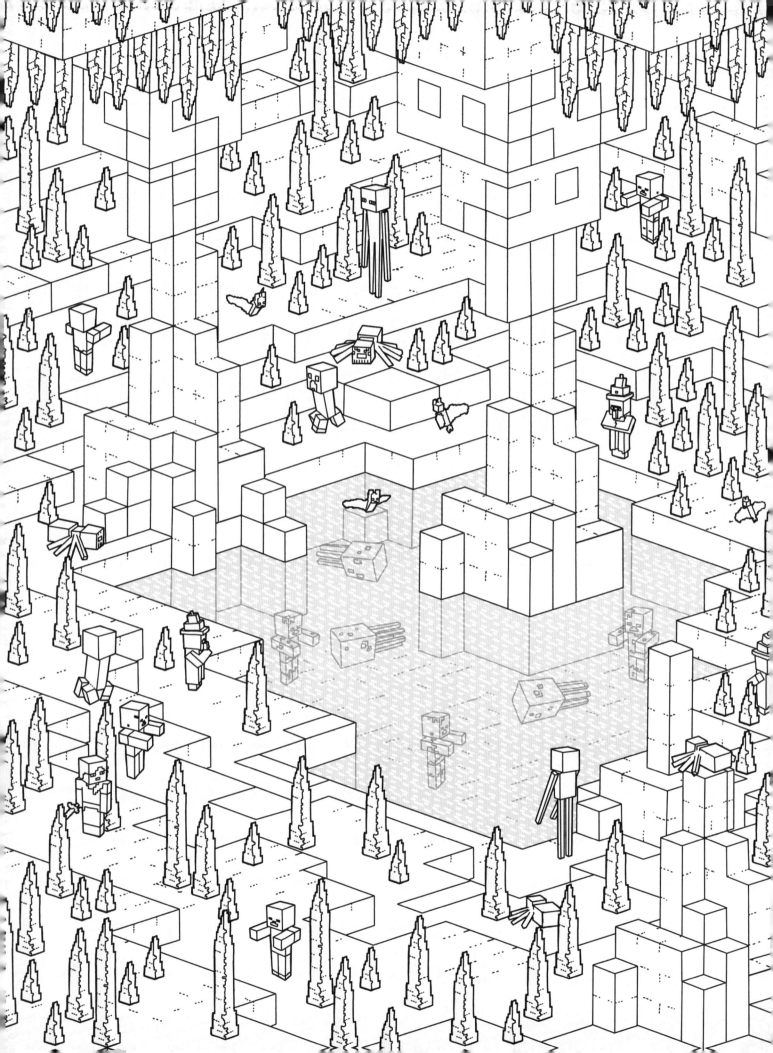

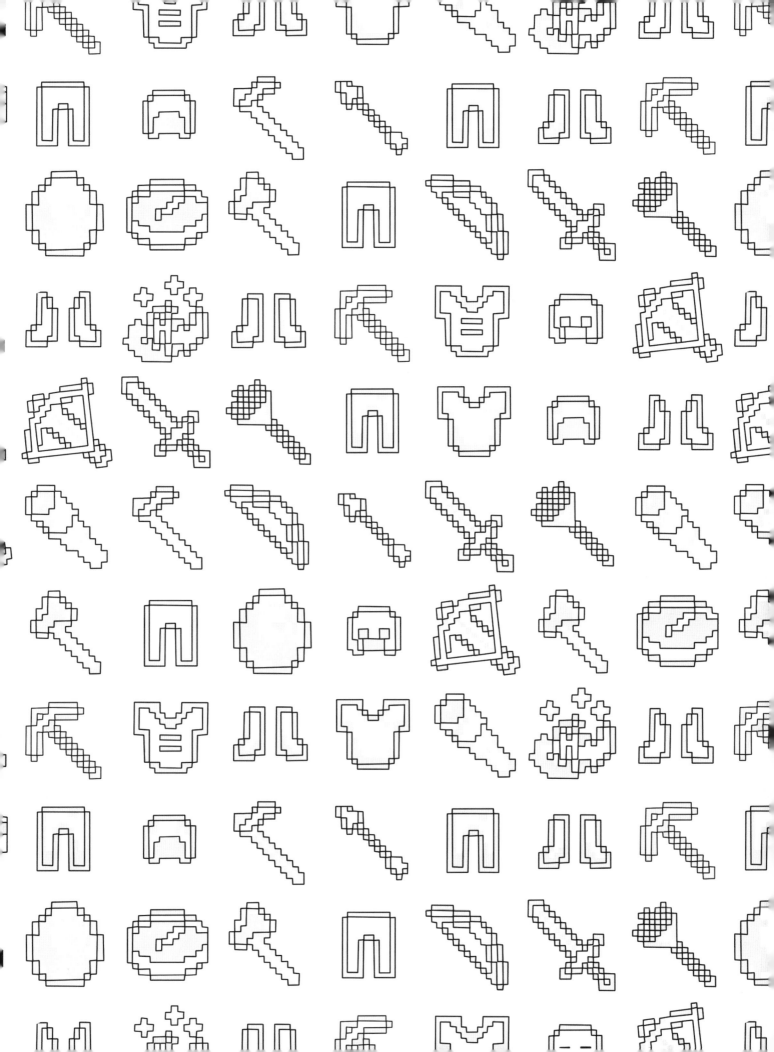

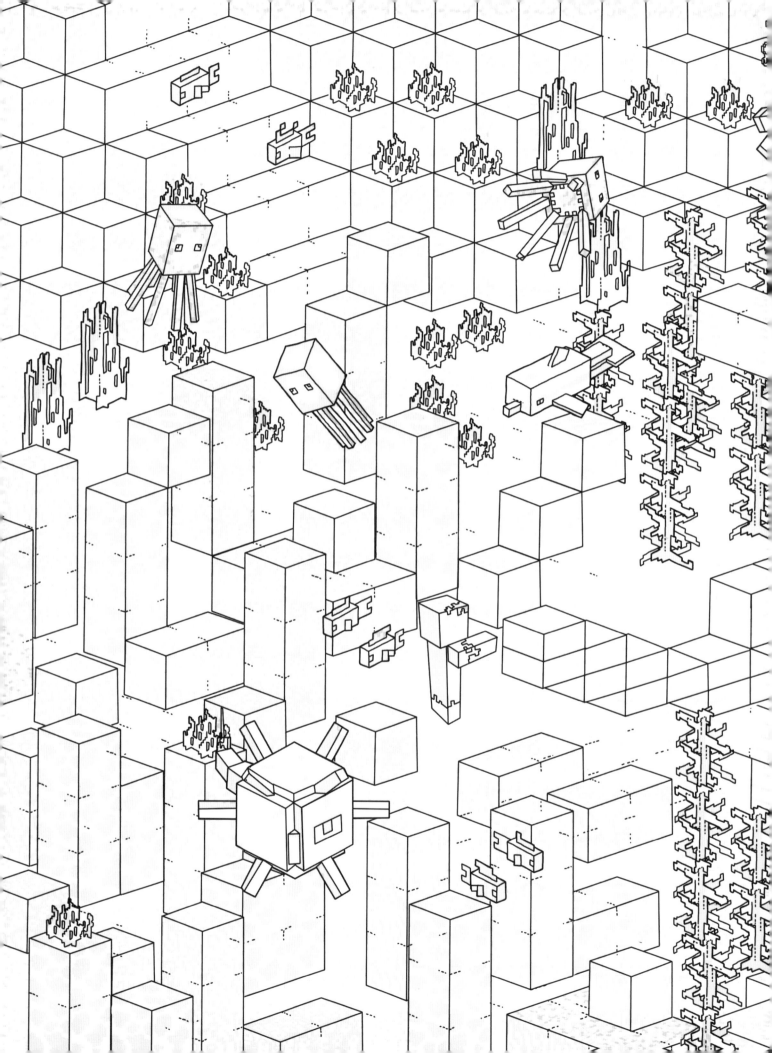

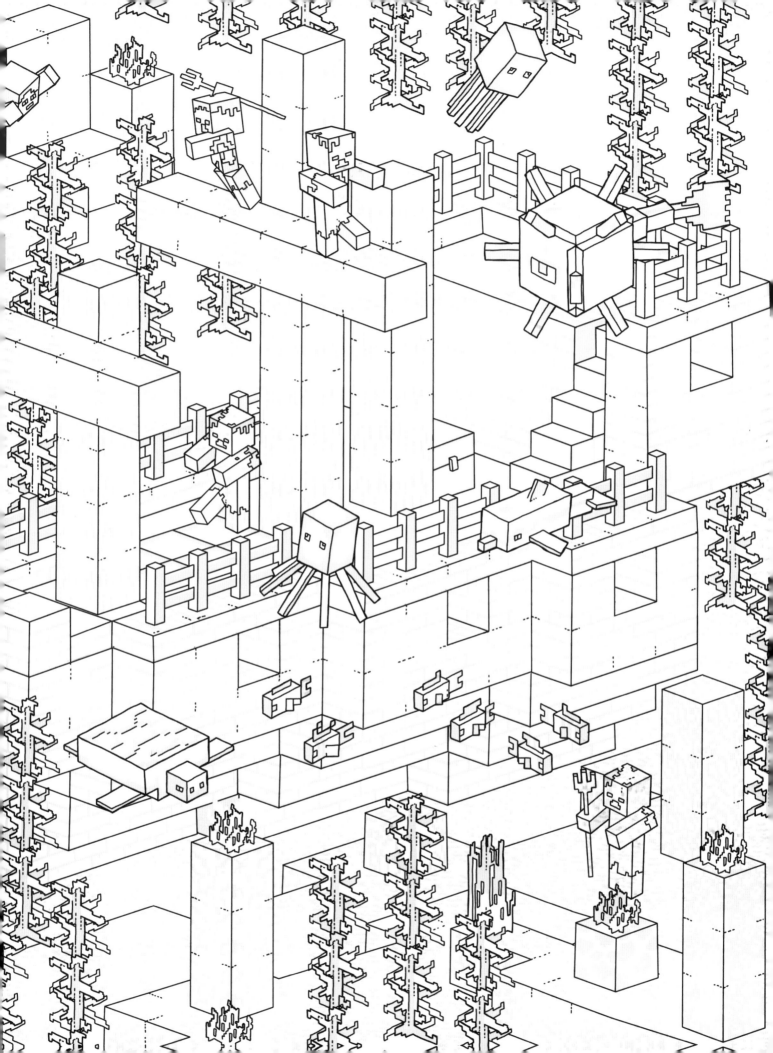

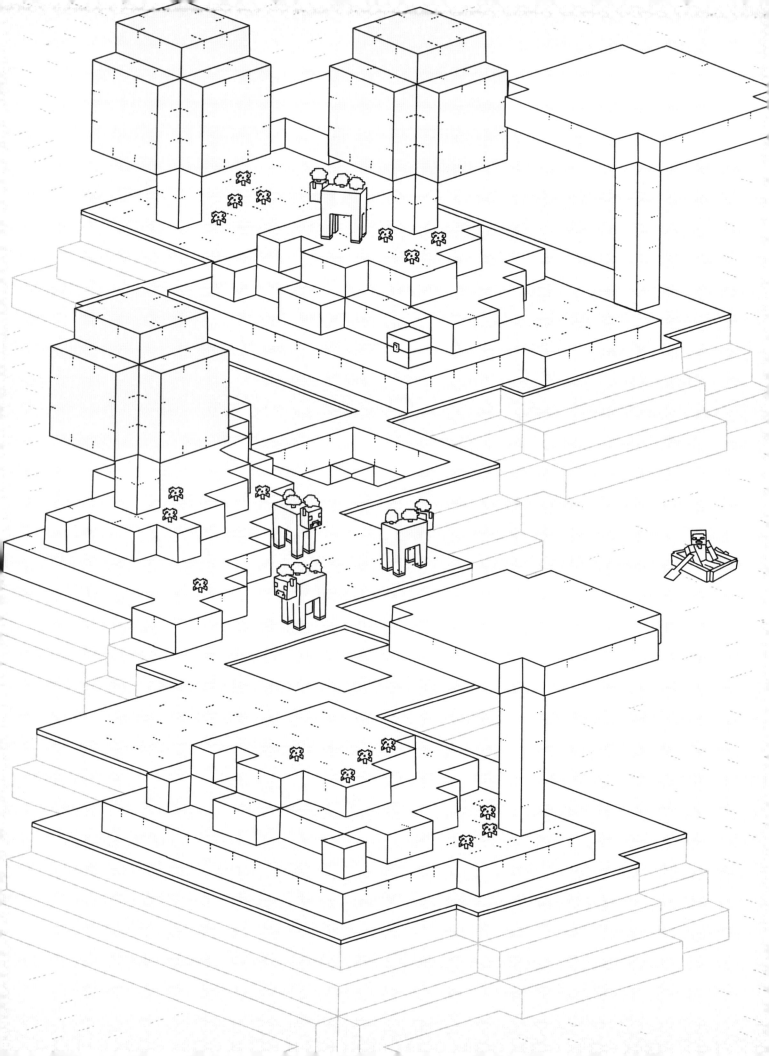

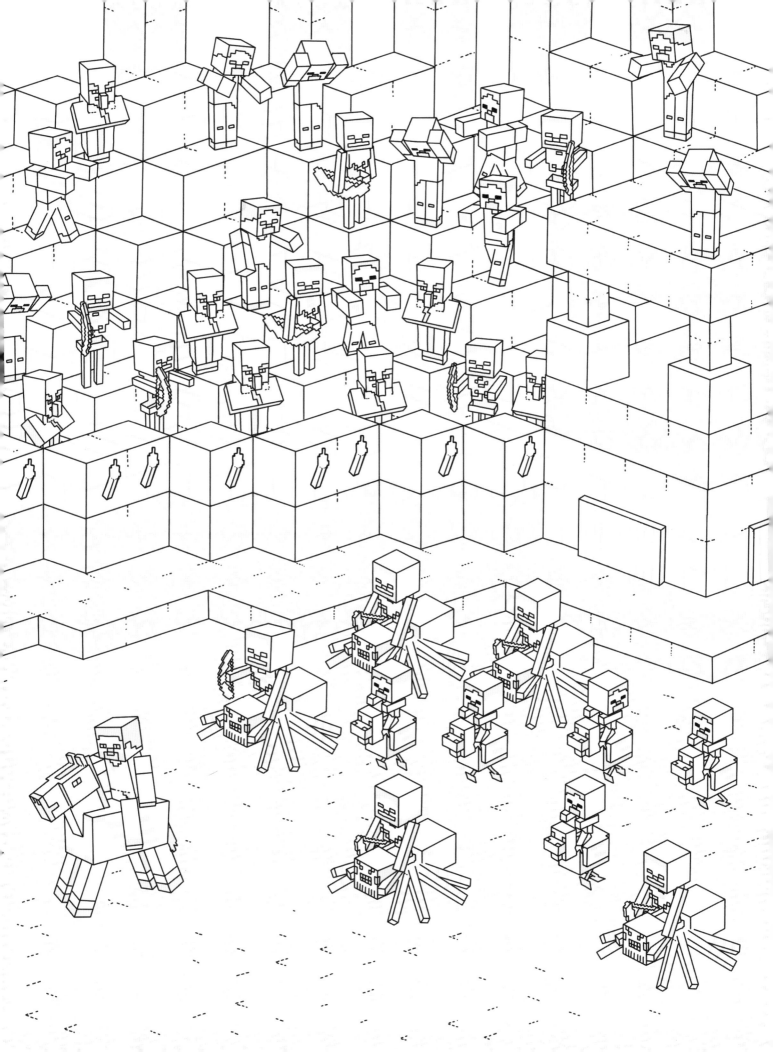

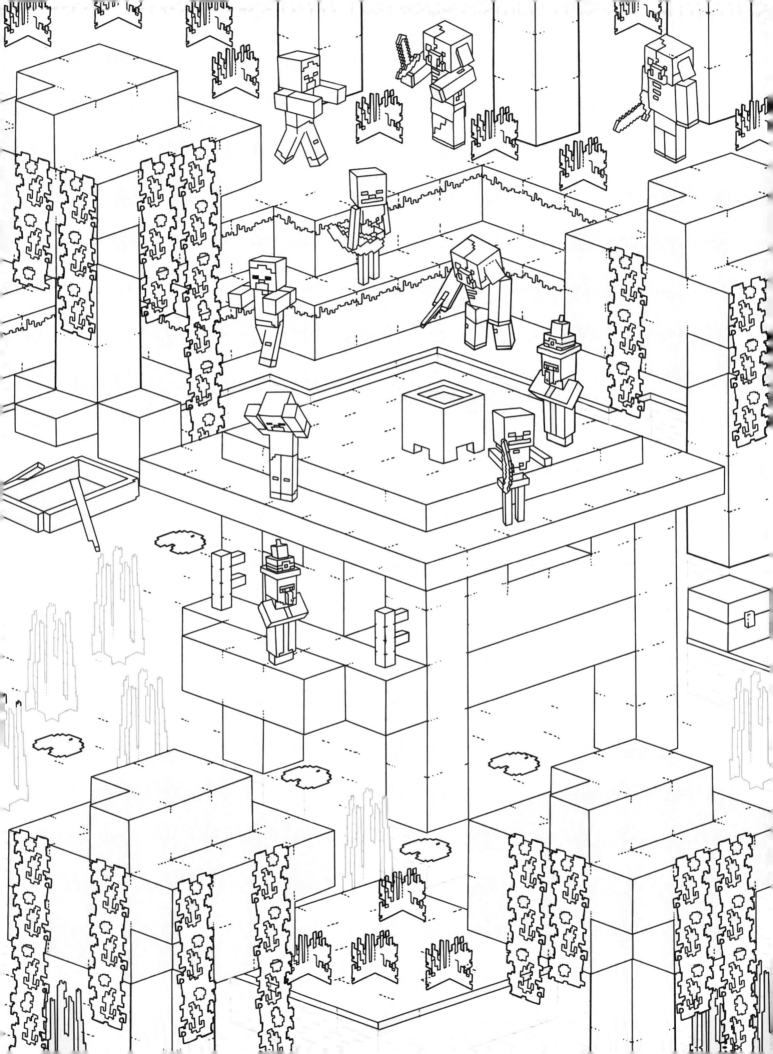

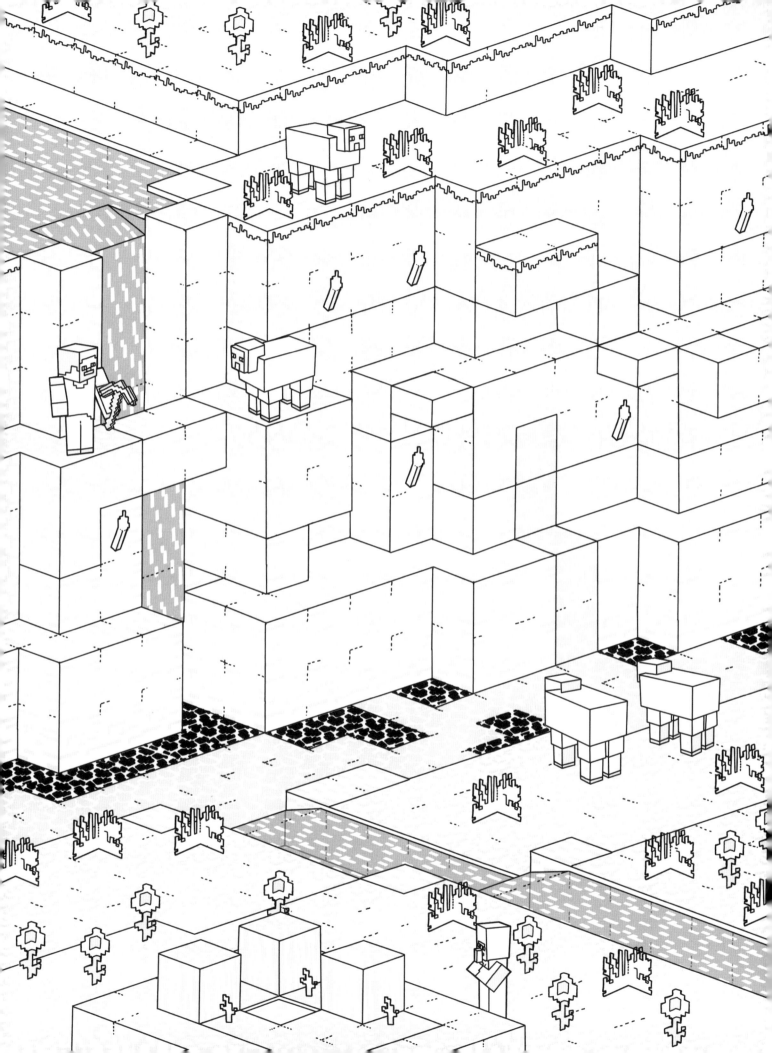

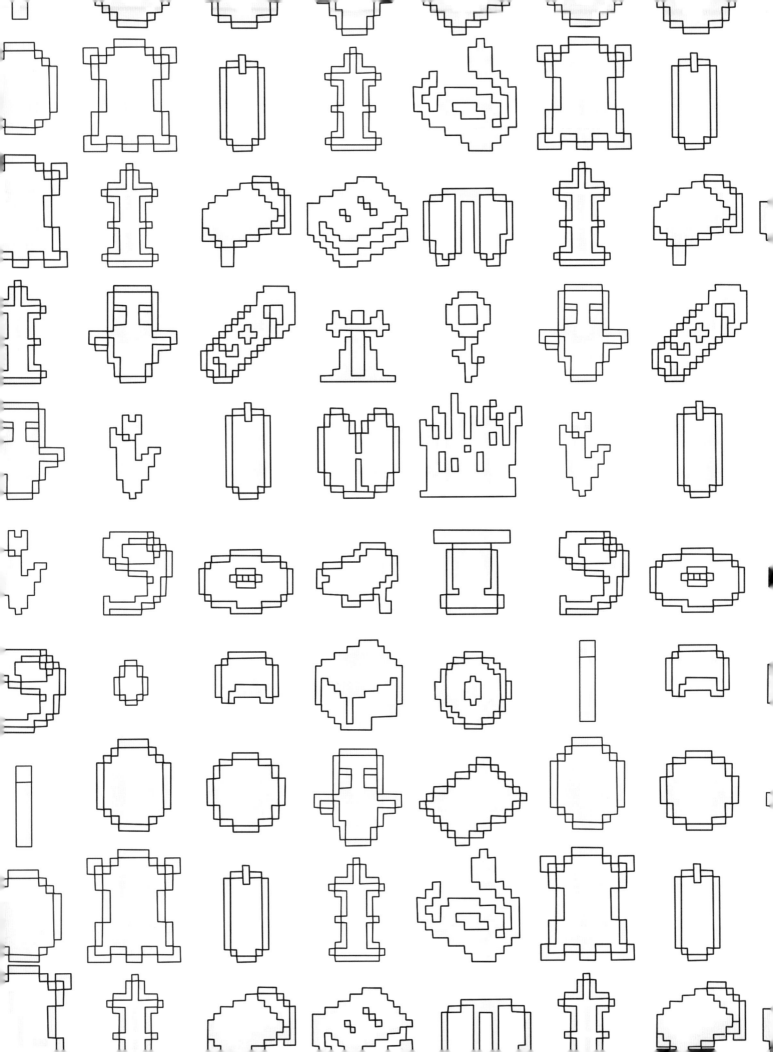

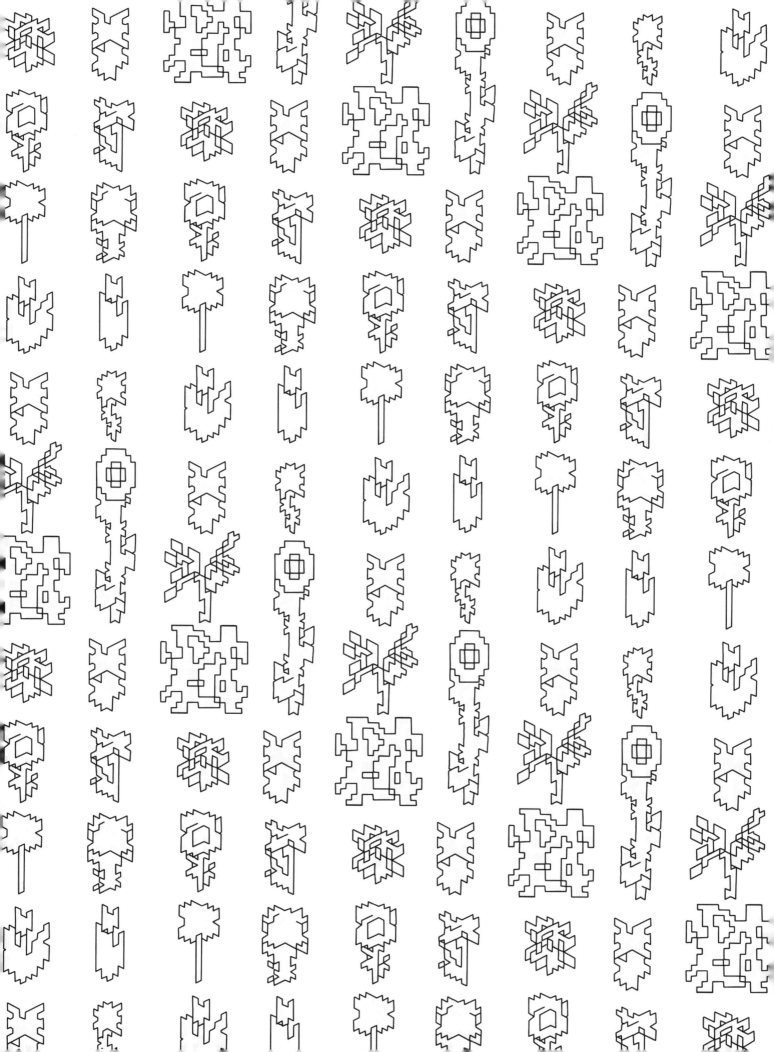

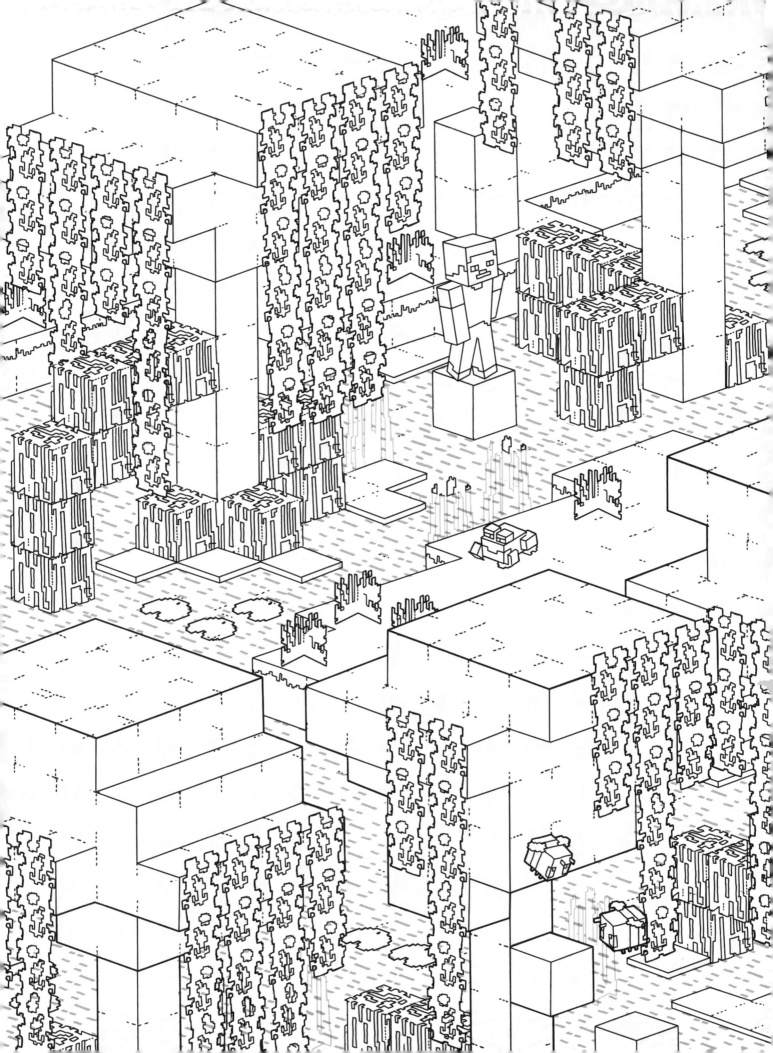

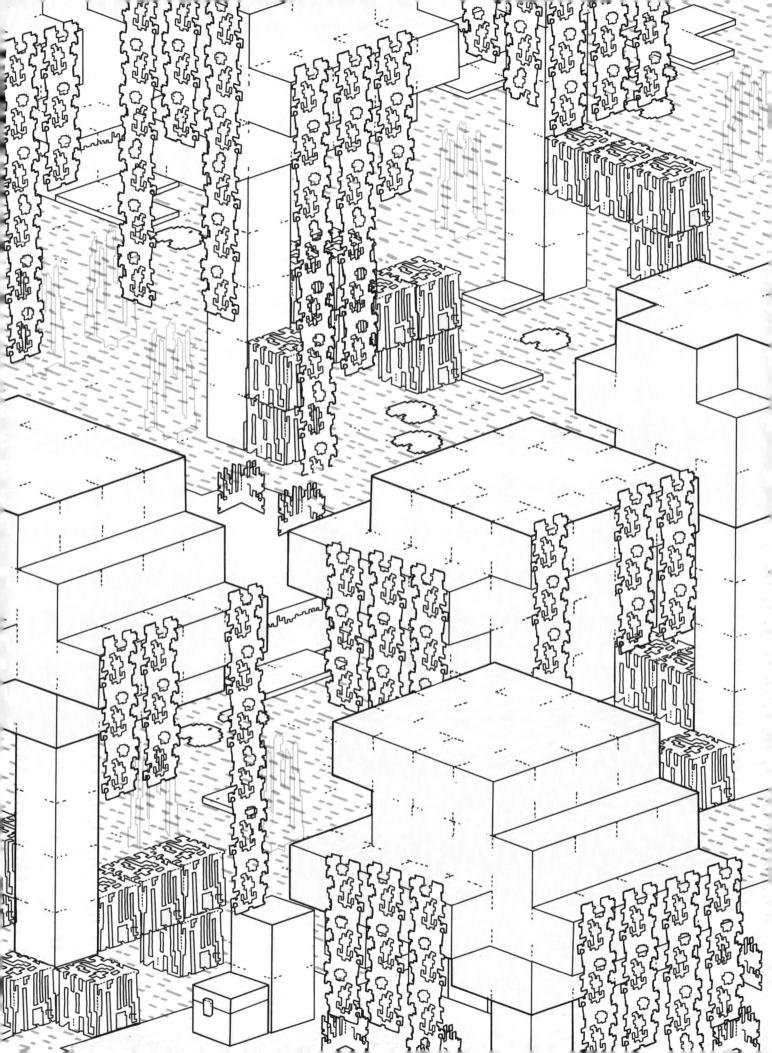

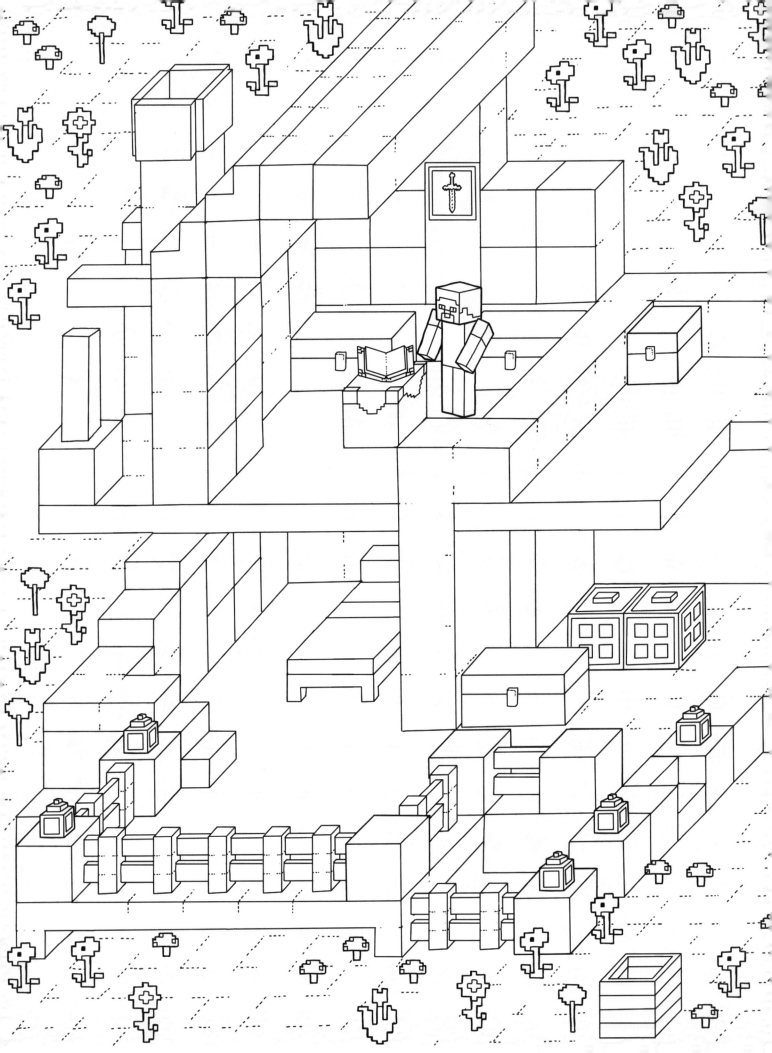

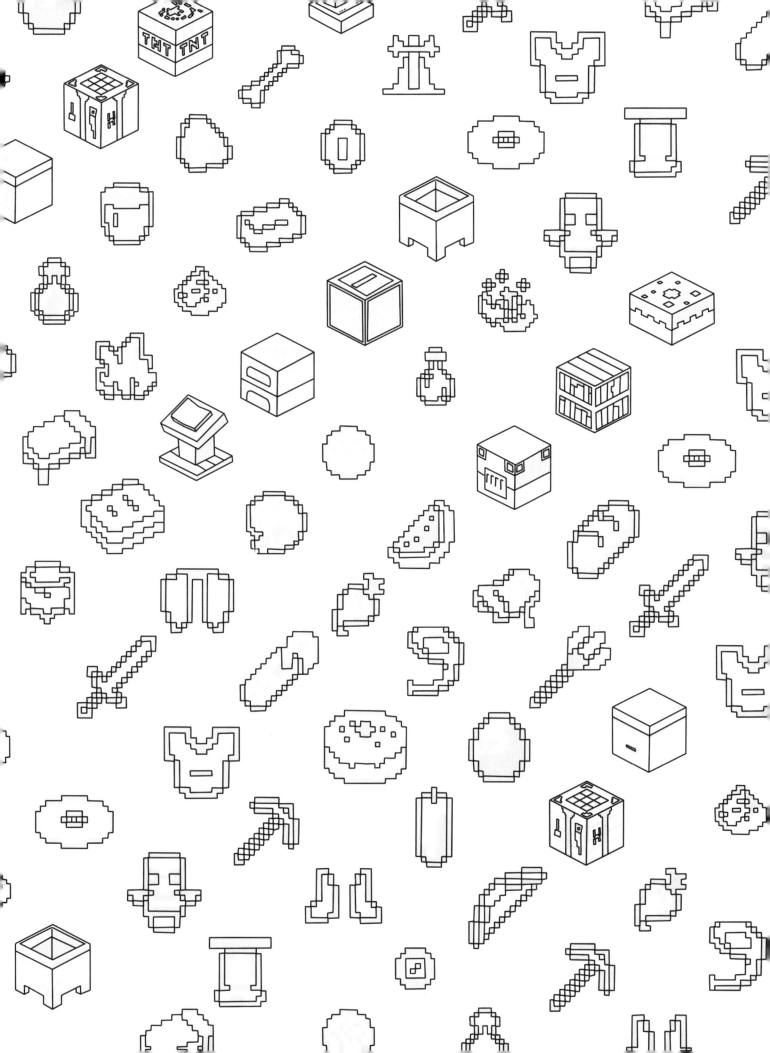

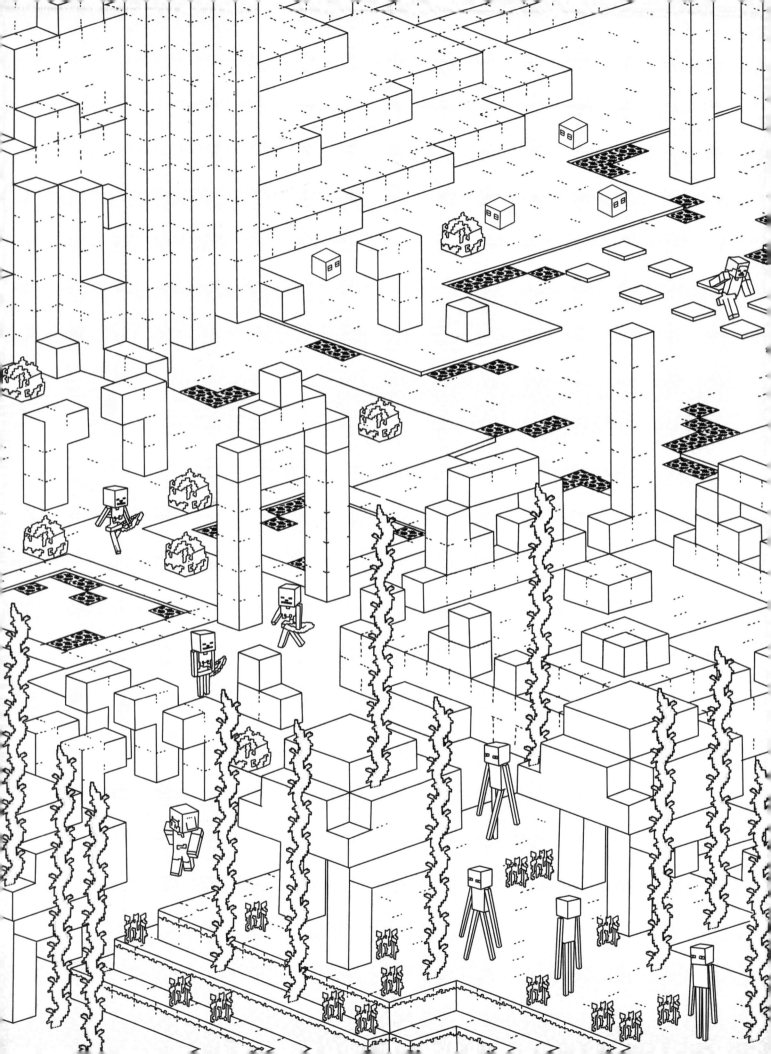

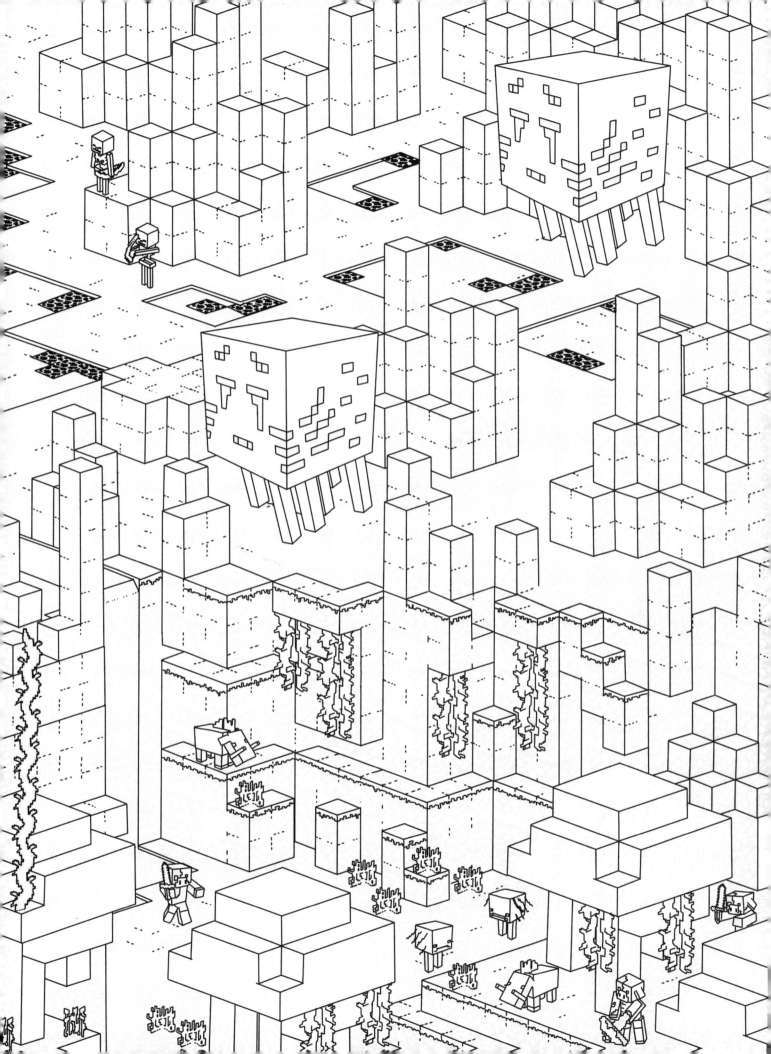

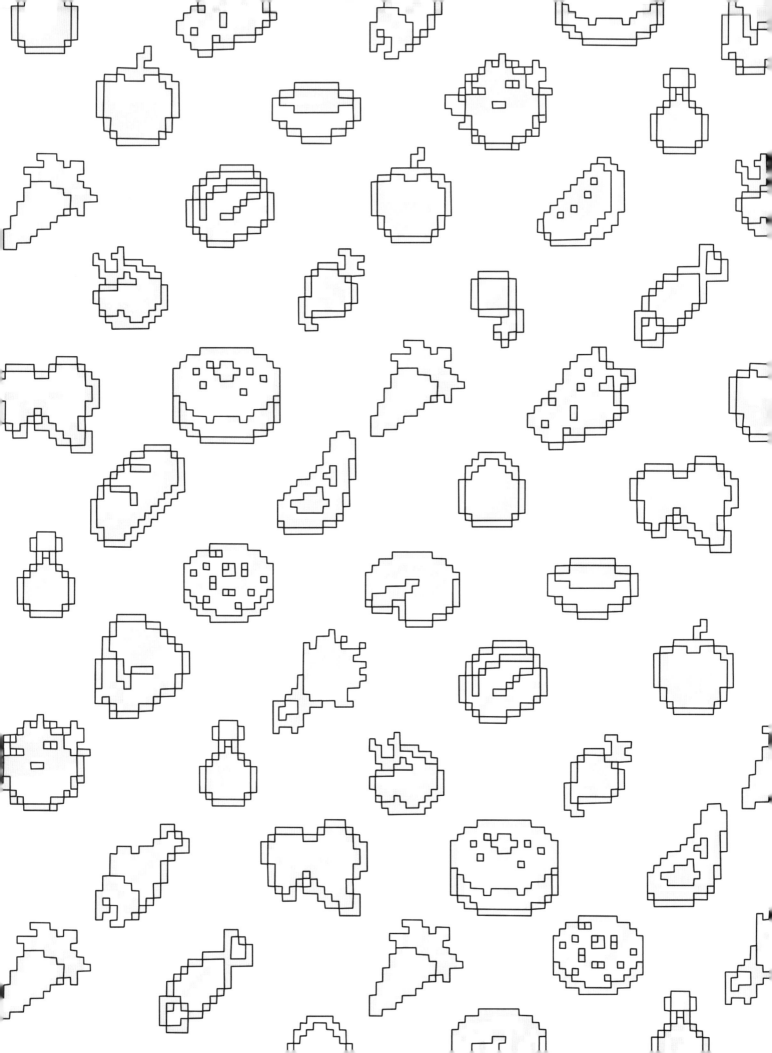

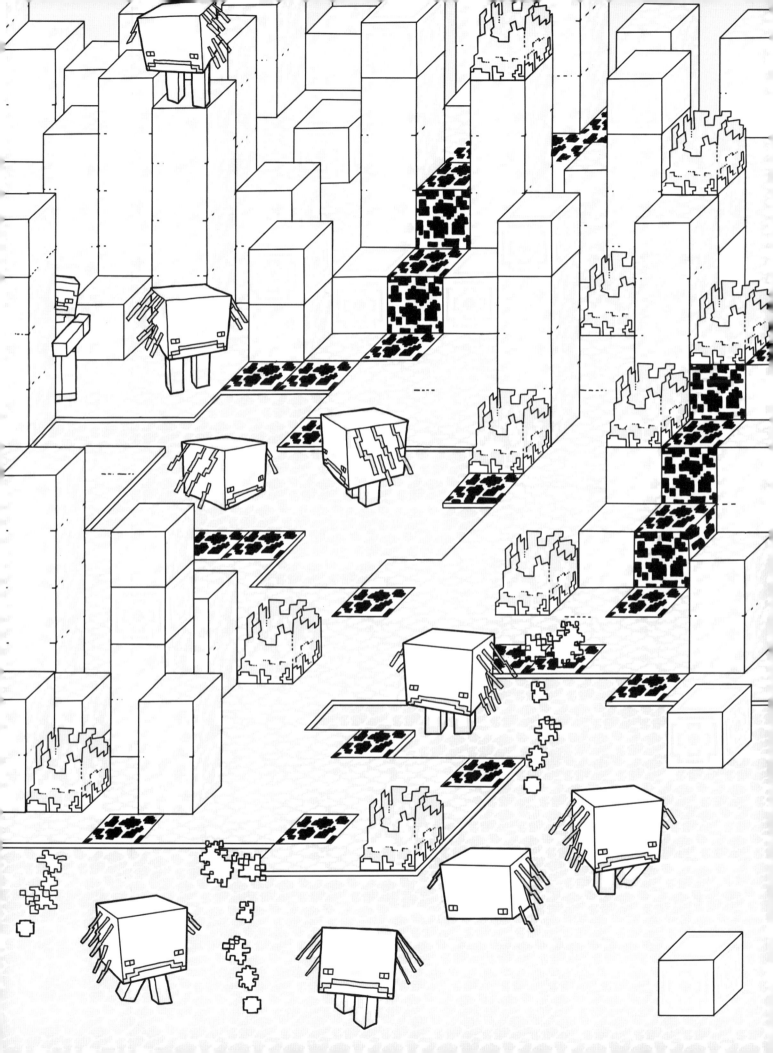

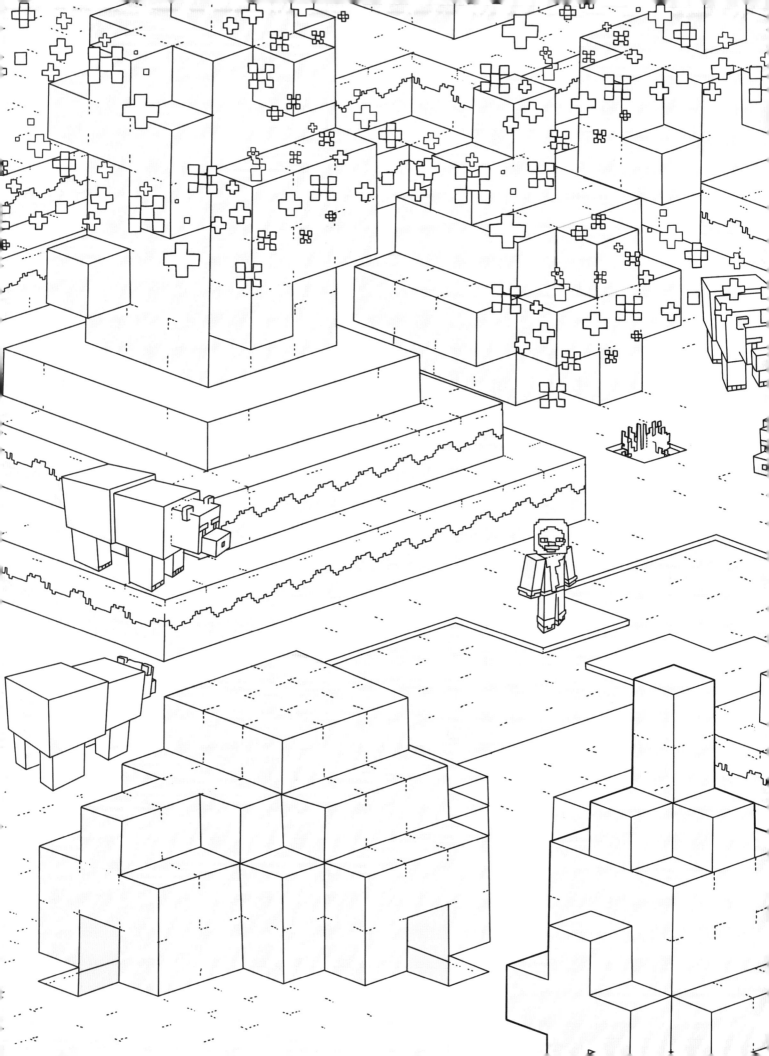

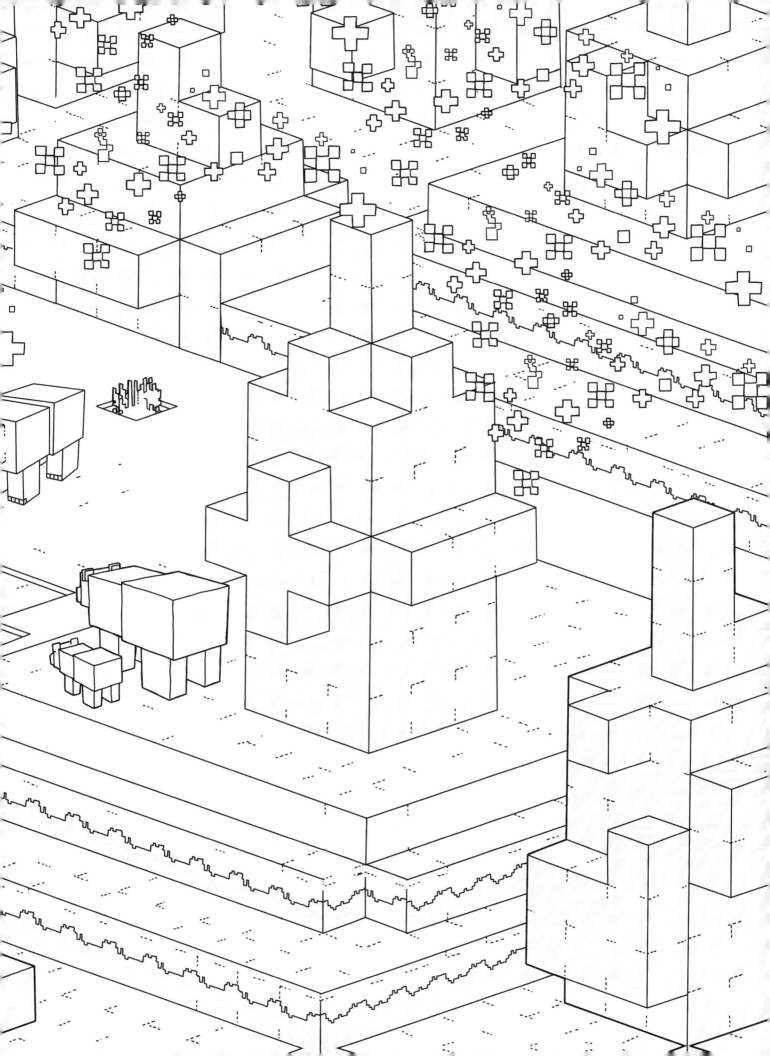

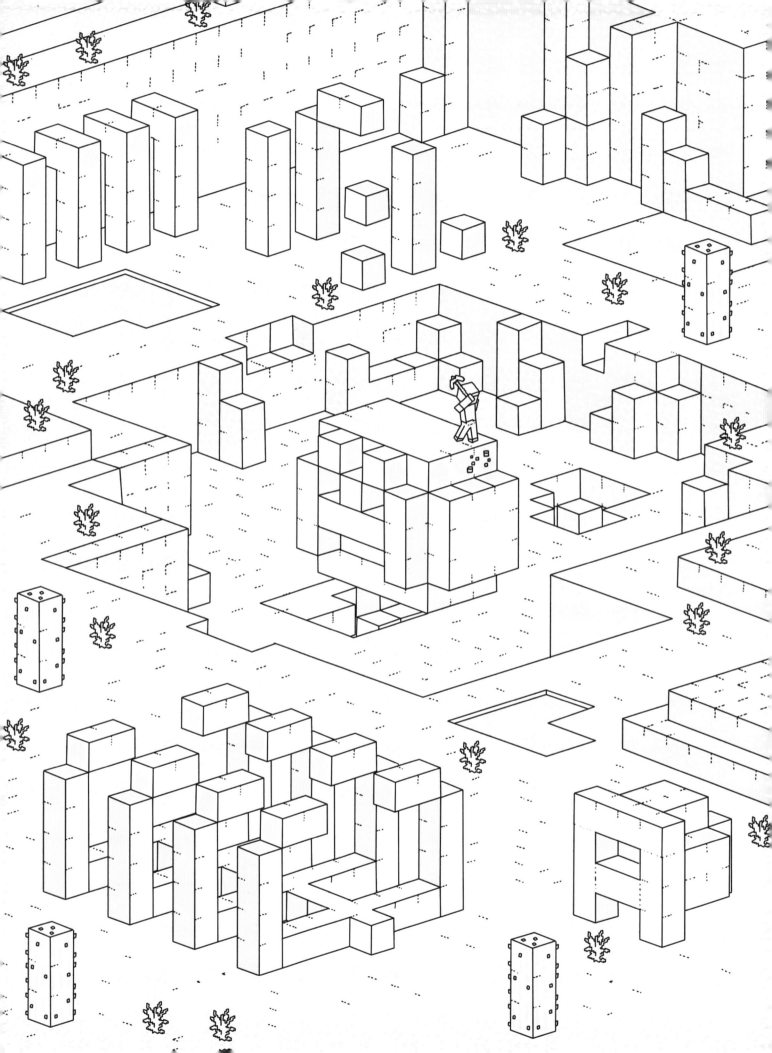

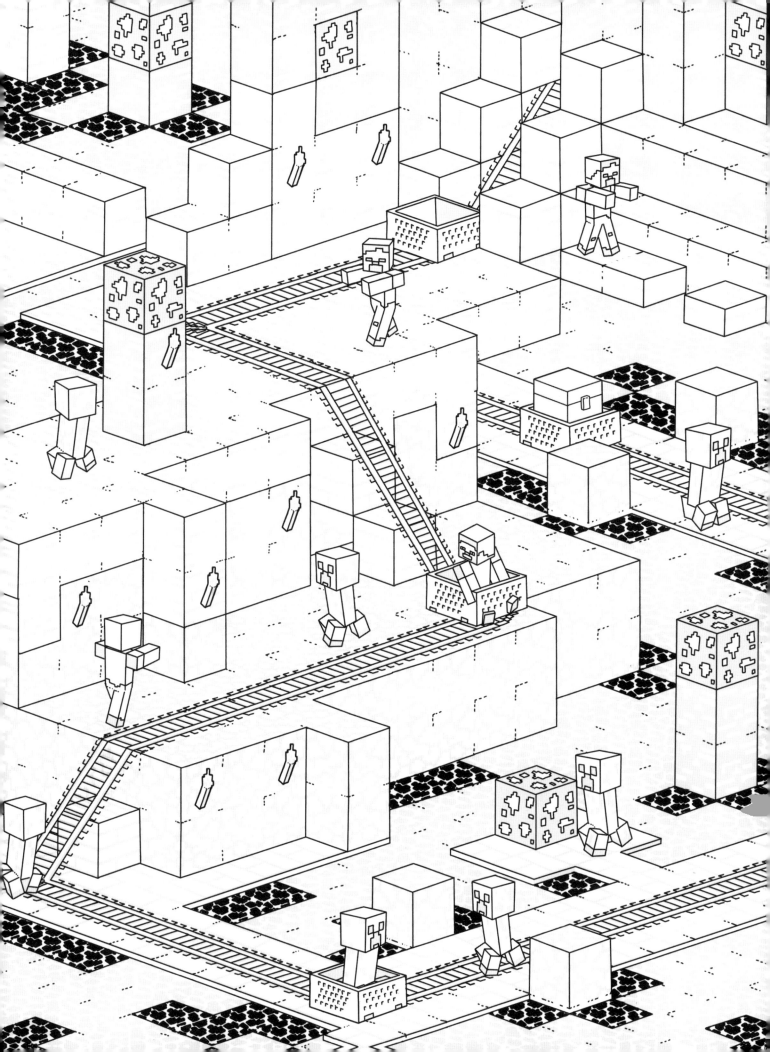

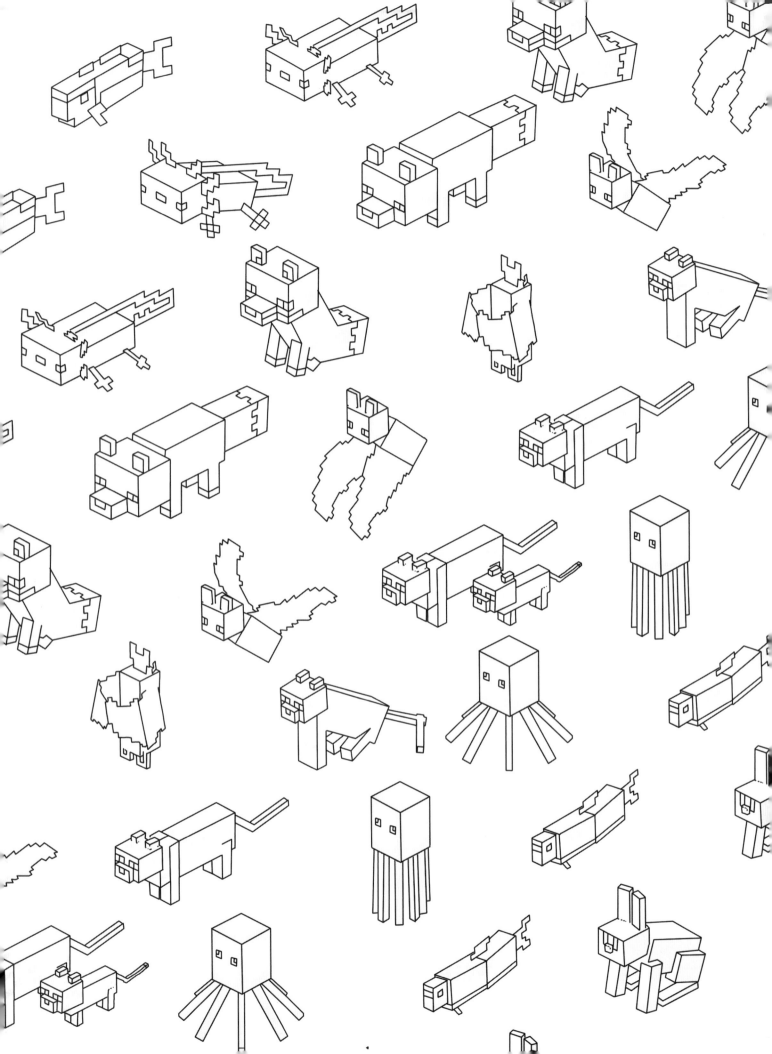

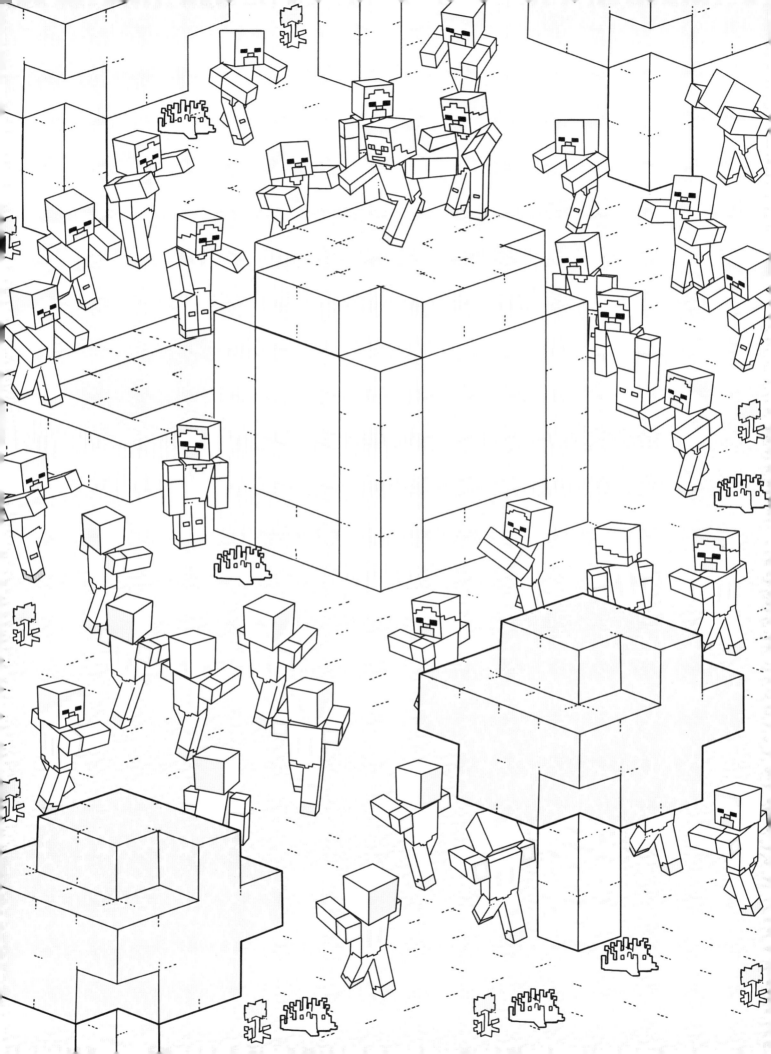

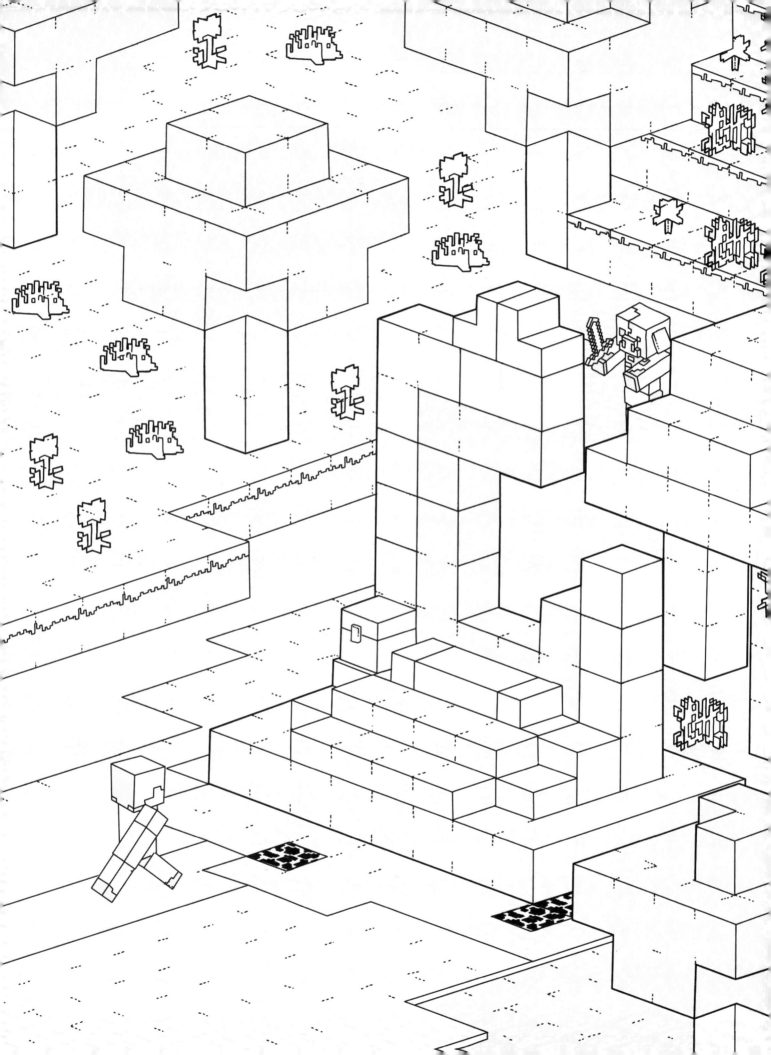

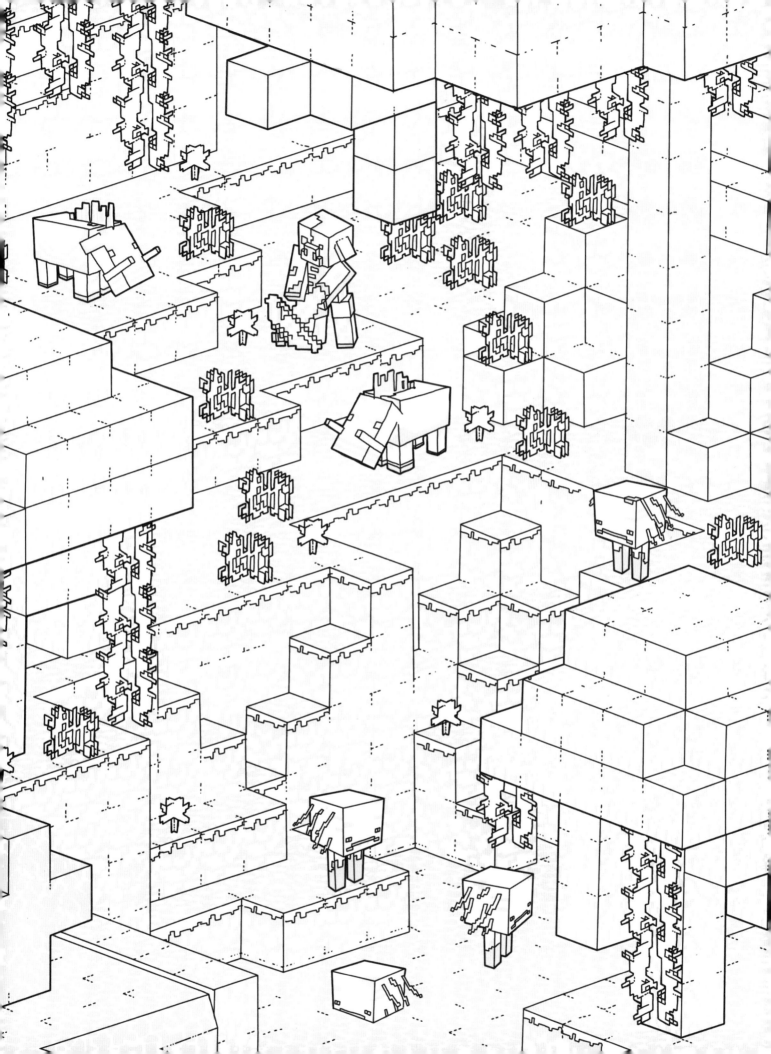

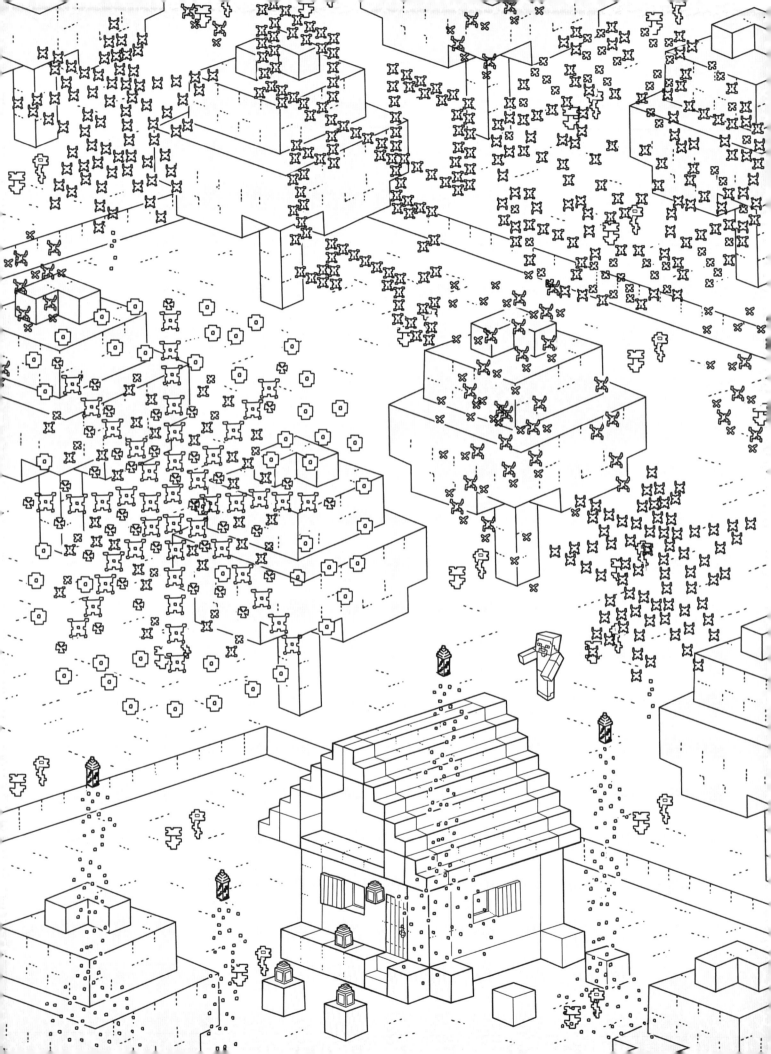

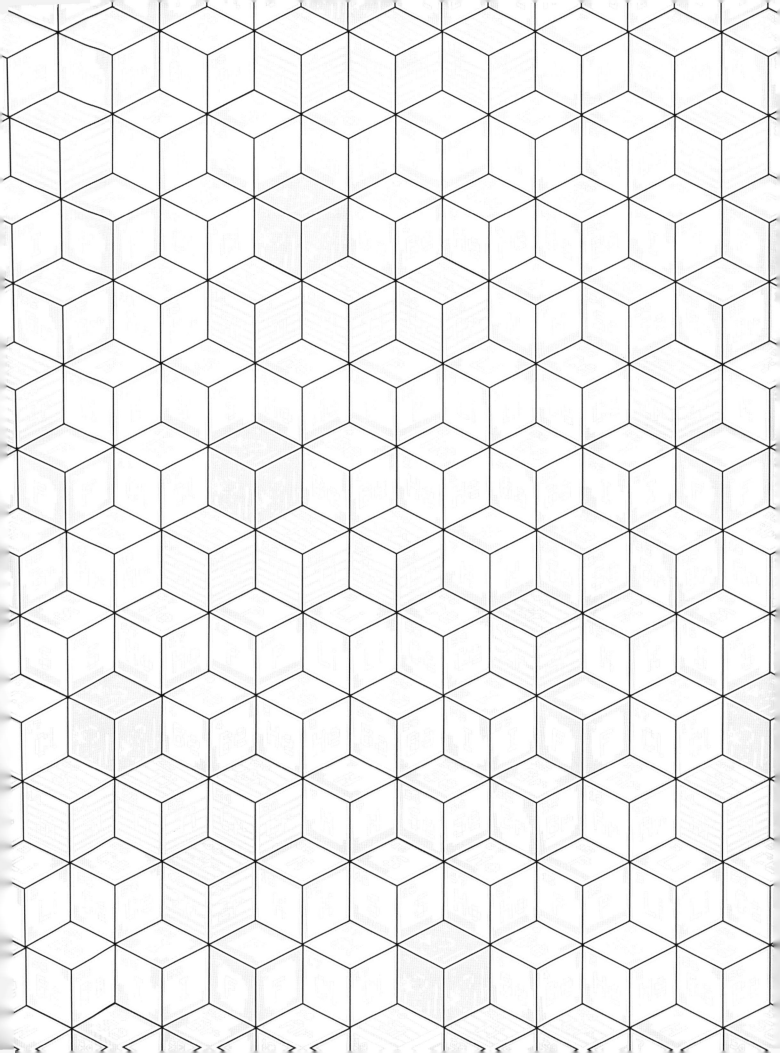

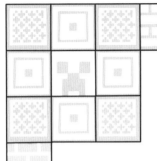

INSIGHT
EDITIONS

PO Box 3088
San Rafael, CA 94912
www.insighteditions.com

Find us on Facebook: www.facebook.com/InsightEditions
Follow us on Twitter: @insighteditions

ISBN: 978-1-64722-699-2

Publisher: Raoul Goff
VP of Licensing and Partnerships: Vanessa Lopez
VP of Creative: Chrissy Kwasnik
VP of Manufacturing: Alix Nicholaeff
VP, Editorial Director: Vicki Jaeger
Publishing Director: Mike Degler
Design Manager: Megan Sinead Harris
Designer: Brooke McCullum
Editor: Anna Wostenberg
Managing Editor: Maria Spano
Senior Production Editor: Katie Rokakis
Production Associate: Tiffani Patterson
Senior Production Manager, Subsidiary Rights: Lina s Palma-Temena

Illustrated by Valentin Ramon
Minecraft Master Builder: Christian Glücklich

Special THANK YOU to Sherin Kwan, Alex Wiltshire,
Audrey Searcy, and the Mojang Team

Hey Minecraft Community!

Make sure to look for
**MINECRAFT: GATHER, COOK,
EAT! OFFICIAL COOKBOOK.**

Available in stores and online.

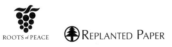

ROOTS of PEACE   REPLANTED PAPER

Insight Editions, in association with Roots of Peace, will plant two trees
for each tree used in the manufacturing of this book. Roots of Peace
is an internationally renowned humanitarian organization dedicated to
eradicating land mines worldwide and converting war-torn lands into
productive farms and wildlife habitats. Roots of Peace will plant two
million fruit and nut trees in Afghanistan and provide farmers there
with the skills and support necessary for sustainable land use.

Manufactured in USA by Insight Editions

10 9 8 7 6